The Complexity and Progression of Black Representation in Film and Television

The Complexity and Progression of Black Representation in Film and Television

David L. Moody

LEXINGTON BOOKS
Lanham • Boulder • New York • London

Published by Lexington Books
An imprint of The Rowman & Littlefield Publishing Group, Inc.
4501 Forbes Boulevard, Suite 200, Lanham, Maryland 20706
www.rowman.com

Unit A, Whitacre Mews, 26-34 Stannary Street, London SE11 4AB

British Library Cataloguing in Publication Information Available

Library of Congress Cataloging-in-Publication Data Available

ISBN: 978-0-7391-8837-8 (cloth : alk. paper)
ISBN: 978-0-7391-8838-5 (electronic)

♾™ The paper used in this publication meets the minimum requirements of American National Standard for Information Sciences Permanence of Paper for Printed Library Materials, ANSI/NISO Z39.48-1992.

Printed in the United States of America

To all the brothers and sisters who have performed on stage, on the tube, and on the silver screen.

Contents

Preface

The Notion of Representation . . . A Few Thoughts

> There is a beam of light spotlighting the figure—part human, identifying ethnicity. Light exposes what is hidden in darkness—however, it also serves as a channel of guidance for footsteps, freedom, and inherited Liberty.
>
> —Rosalind Moody-Lanton

The notion of representation according to Stuart Hall is "the idea of giving." Hall suggests that "representation is the way in which meaning is somewhat given to things depicted . . . through the images or whatever it is on screen, or the words on a page which stands for what we are talking about" (Stuart Hall, *Representation and the Media*, 1997). Today, discussions surrounding the complexity and progression of Black representation in the film, television, and entertainment industries continue to focus on disparaging roles, stereotypes, and the underrepresentation of Black actors in feature films and behind the scenes.

According to a study done by USC's Annenberg School for Communication and Journalism, popular films still provide inadequate representation of minorities in character roles and as directors:

> Popular films still under-represent minority characters and directors, and reflect certain biases in their portrayals. . . . Researchers evaluated 500 top-grossing movies released at the U.S. box office between 2007 and 2012 and 20,000 speaking characters, finding patterns in the way different races, ethnicities and genders are depicted. Hispanic women, the study found, are the demographic most likely to be shown nude or in sexy attire; black men are the group least likely to be portrayed in a committed relationship. (Rebecca Keegan, *Los Angeles Times*, 2013)

The study, which was conducted by Dr. Stacy L. Smith, Marc Choueiti, and Dr. Katherine Pieper, focused on five hundred films from 2007 to 2012 and found that the images portrayed did not reflect the racial and ethnic makeup of American people. According to the study: "Of those speaking characters whose race/ethnicity could be ascertained across 100 top-grossing films of 2012, only 10.8 percent are Black, 4.2 percent are Hispanic, 5 percent are Asian, and 3.6 percent are from other (or mixed race) ethnicities. Just over three-quarters of all speaking characters are White (76.3 percent)" (USC report 2013).

Representation is an opportunity for individuals to make choices (agency), to have a voice, and to speak on someone's behalf. The book cover photograph illustrates an "empty picture"—an image all too familiar and historically often associated with the lack of opportunities for Black Americans on the screen and behind the scenes in film and television.

On July 31, 2009, after I returned from a trip to Finland, I was having dinner with a friend in New York City who happens to be an attorney (as many of you know, attorneys love to analyze everything). Before we called it a night, we decided to stop by the famous "Carnegie Deli" on 7th Avenue at 55th Street for a slice of cheesecake (Carnegie Deli is well known for their cheesecake). A point of interest for most people who dine at Carnegie Deli is the wall of famous photos of celebrities who have also eaten there.

My friend commented there were very few photos of famous African Americans on "The Wall." At the time, he didn't know that I teach courses on minority representation. There were shots of Marilyn Monroe, Frank Sinatra, and David Letterman but no visible images of any Black entertainers (at least at the main entrance of the Deli). He stated, "People come from all over the world to eat here; yet, you don't see many (if any) Black faces on the wall. One could get the impression there are no famous Black people, however, several (famous and not so famous) Blacks have eaten here for many years." I have to chuckle as I think about the characters Sal and Mookie in Spike Lee's movie *Do the Right Thing*. Trust me, we did not throw anything at or through the window. *"It's kind of scary teaching the truth, scary and dangerous"* (*To Sir with Love*, 1967).

Peace, many blessings, and most of all thanks for reading this book and doing "The Right Thing."

Acknowledgments

Special thanks goes out to Stephanie Pritchard for all your hard work editing this project (thank you for taking time to make all those line edits!). To my close friend Dr. Rob Prince Obey—Thanks again my brother! To Kendis Gibson and Jarrod Bunch—Thank you! A big thanks to Colleen Dunham Indexing! I would also like to thank Alison Pavan, Nicolette Amstutz, and Kasey Beduhn (Rowman & Littlefield and Lexington Books)—Thanks for being patient and supporting me on yet another project. To my wonderful, loving Mother—Thanks for bailing me out . . . one more time. Finally, I would like to thank you, the reader.

Introduction

Who Am I?

It is clear to me now that God plays no favorites.

—Acts 10:34 (The Voice)

Who am I?

Am I Brown?
Coffee?
Chocolate?
Tan?
Yes, perhaps tan that resembles
the forbidden desert sand.
When you look at me,
what do you see?
Do I have a puckered brow?
Am I relevant to the here and now?

Who am I?

Am I White?
Would it be okay,
if I said I was an Ofay?
Can I pass for White?
Passing . . .
can I pass?

Who am I?

Am I Yellow?
Fair-haired,
Golden Haired,
Fair . . .
High Yellow,
Low Yellow,
Do you have the fever?
That *Jungle Fever*?
Body temperature RISES
for a White girl.
Body temperature RISES

for a Black boy.
Am I a Negro?
Old school term . . .
Dates back to the 50s.
Am I Colored?
Old school term . . .
dates back to the 50s.
Person of Color?
Might work.
Post Mod term . . .
Post Mod World.
Might work.
Not everyone, not everybody, wants to be called
Negro.
African American.
Nigger.
Nigga.

Who am I?

Am I Black? Black is beautiful!
So they say.
Black is BEAUTIFUL!
Black Arts Movement, Blaxploitation, *Soul Train*, BET,
so they say.
Say it Loud, I'm Black and I'm Proud . . .
Say what?
BLACK IDENITY
THE REVOLUTION! THE REVOLUTION!
So they say.

Who Am I?
When you look at me, what do you think?
When you look at me, what do you see?
Buffoon.
Baboon.
Black Mammy.
Black Buck.
Trickster.
"Black F**k."
Slave.
Pimp.
Con.
Addict.
Hoodlum.
Gangster Rapper.
Nappy Head.
Welfare Recipient.
Low Self-Esteem.

Problem Child.
Queer.
Child of God . . .

Who am I?

Amen.

—David L. Moody

ONE

Race Films as a Genre in American Cinema

"Now performing, An All-Star Colored Cast"

From the very beginning of the early stages in American cinema, African Americans had a presence on the silver screen. The twentieth century created a new era of cinema that consisted of films produced for and targeted to an all-Black audience. "Race films," which existed in the United States for over thirty years (1913–1948), were films produced by African Americans that focused on Black themes and highlighted the talents of African American directors, producers, scriptwriters, and actors.[1]

However, according to African American film scholar Thomas Cripps, these early films were not truly Black because their functions, more or less, were to enlighten and mollify White people's curiosity concerning Black culture. The argument presented by Cripps creates an opportunity for speculation on how to categorize a well-known group of films about Black people that in most cases included the participation of White filmmakers.[2] How do we define the term "race film"? Moreover, can these films be considered a "genre" or are they imitations of similar narratives produced by White filmmakers such as comedies, dramas, and musicals? Furthermore, were race films merely exploiting issues pertaining to skin color and class status? In this chapter I examine why the term "race film" is obscure while exploring the criteria often used to label a film within a particular category or genre.

In his book *Black Film as Genre*, Thomas Cripps illustrates how difficult it is to provide an acceptable definition of Black cinema. Cripps posits a notion of "Black film" that refers to

those motion pictures made for theater distribution that have a black
producer, director, and writer, or black performers; that speak to black
audiences or, incidentally, to white audiences posed of preternatural
curiosity, attentiveness, or sensibility toward racial matters; and that
emerge from self-conscious intentions, whether artistic or political, to
illuminate the Afro-American experience. (3)

Problematic for Cripps is how genre film has been used as a "fabricated
systematic means of examining film" (vii). Cripps calls attention to the
fact that historically, genres of Black cinema emulate those of the White
Hollywood cinema. Examples would include Black musicals (*The St.
Louis Blues*, 1958); films with religious themes (*The Blood of Jesus*, 1941);
documentaries (*The Negro Soldier*, 1944); melodramas (*The Scar of Shame*,
1927); and dramas that thematically dealt with generational issues (*Broken Strings*, 1940, starring Clarence Muse). Black representations were also
visible in Black Westerns such as *The Bronze Buckaroo* (1939), *Harlem Rides
the Range* (1939), and *Harlem on the Prairie* (1937).

The criteria for defining Black film includes: the self-conscious Black
artists who were interested in the medium as an effective tool for delivering a message; those Black artists whose work become known through
conventional channels of production that were supported by White finances; and finally (though according to Cripps it was rare), films produced by White filmmakers whose work attracted the attention, if not the
unconditional praise, of Black movie goers and critics (4). Cripps suggests that because of assimilation (which would include the participation
of White filmmakers) the term "race film" becomes problematic. Moreover, given Cripps's definition, the term "Black film" must be seen as a
genre, based on what it says and how it is said, rather than who is saying
it (9). Therefore, "Black film" becomes a more inclusive term when referring to a body of work about Black people.

SEGREGATED CINEMA OF THE EARLY 1900s

According to Black popular culture scholar Michele Wallace, the crucial
development in the history of Black performance was when stereotypical
images went from derisive drawings to photographs (after the mid-
1890s) into film footage. The footage consisted of Black people engaged in
the perennially American performance of Blackness in part for a White
audience but also, as well, for a Black audience (486). In the early 1900s,
the only film images of Blacks were degrading depictions that featured
White actors in Blackface (such as Mammies, Coons, and White actors
speaking in a plantation dialect) and reduced Black entertainment value
on film to the lowest common denominator (Berry, 7).

Previous arguments regarding the evolution of race films focused on a
discourse that suggested these films were produced as a rebuttal to racist

themes projected in D. W. Griffith's controversial film *Birth of a Nation*. However, akin to Thomas Cripps, film scholar Jane Gaines raises a question regarding what motivated the Black filmmaker to produce Black films before the 1915 production of *Birth of a Nation*. Before *Birth of a Nation*, films such as *The Masher* (1907) and *The Wooing Wedding of the Coon* (1907) featured White actors in Blackface that portrayed African Americans in demeaning character roles. Given the negative images of African Americans on the silver screen and the segregation concerns in America, I contend that Black identity and self-esteem issues were the primary motivators for the development of a Black aesthetic and voice by the early Black auteur.

In *Fire & Desire: Mixed-Race Movies in the Silent Era*, Gaines states that during the silent era, American cinema was defined by two separate and parallel industries, with White and Black companies producing films for their respective, segregated audiences (127). Given the impossibility of purity and the co-implication of White and Black, Gaines explores the cinematic constitution of identity by examining the positive images of the "New Negro" (127). Since the later part of the nineteenth century, the reconstruction of a positive public image for African Americans has been a continuous yet difficult challenge. According to Gaines, the construct of the New Negro was a crusade launched by the literary work of Frederick Douglass, Paul Lawrence Dunbar, Charles Chestnutt, and W. E. B. Du Bois.[3] Du Bois raises the critical question regarding the reconstruction of Black identity and the impossibility of purity within any given art form. Du Bois asserts:

> The Negro is sort of seventh son, born with a veil, and gifted with second-sight in this American world—a world which yields him no true self-consciousness, but only lets him see himself through the revelation of the other world. It is a peculiar sensation, this double-consciousness, this sense of always looking at one's self through the eyes of others, measuring one's soul by the tape of a world that looks on in amused contempt and pity. One ever feels his two-ness-an American, a Negro; two souls, two thoughts, two unreconciled strivings; two warring ideals in one dark body, whose dogged strength alone keeps it from being torn asunder. (3)

Gaines contends that by looking at the history of early African American cinema after *Birth of a Nation*, one will see the appearance of a New Negro through the creation of Black owned film companies.

Because of the overwhelming African American critical response to Griffith's film (which included responses ranging from denunciations in the Black press to organized protests around the country) what's lost in the discourse is the fact that Blacks produced and distributed their own films before the release of *Birth of a Nation* in 1915. Gaines states, "So dominate is *Birth of a Nation* in the historical memory of this period that the idea of black-produced motion pictures before Griffith's cinematic provocation is almost unimaginable by whites and, although probably imaginable by blacks, may be completely unfamiliar to them" (93). By placing emphasis on the Black response to Griffith's film, one accentuates only the distinctiveness of Black motion picture production at the cost of seeing commonalities between White and Black filmmakers. "Being aware of the similarities means acknowledging that Black directors and actors wanted to make movies for some of the same reasons that Whites went into the business, and many of the same economic conditions that encouraged White successes made Black enterprises almost impossible" (Gaines, 94). Gaines's analysis of economic achievement directs my attention to the efforts of one particular Black filmmaker, William Foster, who may have produced, written, and directed the first Black film in 1913.

THE BLACK PRESS AND BLACK CINEMA: WILLIAM FOSTER, AKA "JULI JONES"

William Foster, whose introduction to motion pictures came through the theater, worked as a business manager at Chicago's Peking Theater. The Peking Theater was founded during a period when most White Americans believed that Blacks had little or no talent when it came to any type of arts management. Foster is credited as being the first African American filmmaker, and his first film, *The Railroad Porter*, was a two reel comedy in the slap-stick style of Mack Sennett's *Keystone Cops*. Foster's film opened in Chicago at the States and Grand theaters and later was exhibited with the first Black newsreel featuring images of the YMCA parade. Due to the film's success, Foster began to pursue sites for building a studio and to investigate distribution possibilities with Kalem, Lubin, and Pathe, which were White companies located in Jacksonville, Florida. Foster's accomplishments not only signaled an intervention in dominant filmmaking practices, his efforts led to the creation of one of America's first Black owned film companies—Foster Photoplay Company.[4]

Foster's creative abilities and savvy business practices were not just limited to theater and film. He was a talented writer (his pen name was Juli Jones) whose connection with the Black newspaper *The Chicago Defender* reflects the early attempts to establish mass communication vehicles in growing Black urban centers (Gaines, 95). Gaines states, "In his ties with *The Chicago Defender*, Foster illustrates what was distinctive about the early African American film industry" (95). Black newspapers were a strong support system for the early Black filmmakers.[5] According to Anna Everett, "The modern Black press offered both a critical response to and generative mechanism for these pioneering efforts on the eve of America's post-Great War boom years" (111). Everett suggests that because of the separation of races based on the legally mandated Jim Crow laws, the emergence of the Black press network and Black cinema movement evolved from the need to fill the information and entertainment gaps experienced by a dislocated and downtrodden population. A bond was formed within this paradigm between the Black cinema movement and the growing Black press network.

Early on, African American writers and journalists recognized the liberating potential of the basis cinematic apparatus, particularly if protected from the racist imperatives of White production houses. Everett puts forward the notion that as early as 1913, the Black press set in motion a high-profile campaign to publicize and celebrate the abuse of upstart Black filmmakers dedicated to the creation of cinematic images of Blackness that authenticated African American progress and development. Consequently, Everett asserts, "newspaper headlines promoting Black participation in the business of filmmaking were often privileged over the more frequent reactionary headlines railing against mainstream cinema's institutionalized racism" (112). Furthermore, she states that when necessary, both types of film headlines and articles would be strategically placed side by side.[6]

According to Charlene Regester, during 1910–1950, film histories, indexes, filmographies, trade journals, and magazines only occasionally referred to African American contribution to film (1). Regester states, "In the era of segregation, the second-class status of blacks was reflected not only in their screen roles and assignments, but also in the coverage afforded them, with many African Americans in the motion picture industry remaining totally unknown or ignored" (1). Regester points out that the achievement of African Americans in American cinema is found almost exclusively in Black newspapers. The four newspapers chosen for her bibliography are: the *Chicago Defender*, the *Afro-American* (Baltimore), the *Los Angeles Sentinel*, and the *New York Amsterdam News*. The press played an important role in encouraging African Americans to assert themselves in the industry by becoming actors, actresses, filmmakers, producers, directors, and technicians (Regester, 34). Moreover, the aim of these newspapers was to discredit the negative screen representations by submitting the works of Black filmmakers as more authentic visions of Black Americans' adroitness and ambitions.

ANALYSIS OF *THE SCAR OF SHAME*: MELODRAMA OR SOCIAL DRAMA?

"Filmic genre, like literary genre before it, is also permeable to historical and social tension. Some films explicitly connect class and genre" (Stam, 14–15). A popular art that was embraced by the African American community during the early 1900s was the social drama. According to Thomas Cripps, the social drama was a "vehicle for Afro-American sentiment" during the early developments of Black cinema (65). Targeted at an African audience that was at odds with its circumstances, Black social dramas were empathetic to the difficulties of Black social life and served as the medium for expressing Black aspirations (Cripps, 65). Cripps opts to use the term "social drama" versus "melodrama" with respect to the film's narrative. This choice is problematic for Cripps because of how the term "melodrama" is used as a vehicle to address serious social issues within the African American community. In the spirit of conventional melodrama, Cripps argues that Alvin Hilliard's character's course of action towards the end of the film (Hilliard is a principal character role) stands as a flaw within the storyline because conventional melodrama plot structure would not permit a romantic hero to be responsible for a death (74). Cripps states, *"The Scar of Shame* (1927) cannot be judged as an ordinary melodrama. The incidents of plot, setting, and character are [too] dense with social meanings that provide visual signals through which a sensitive viewer perceives an anatomy of Black social life and the social message beneath the contrived plot" (74).[7] The social message beneath what Cripps refers to as a contrived plot merits a closer examination at this point.

The Scare of Shame, which was produced by the White owned Colored Players Film Corporation (CPFC), focuses on two critical issues that existed within the African American community: class and the color caste system of the Black middle class. The story builds on the relationship of a promising Black concert pianist Alvin Hilliard's unequally yoked marriage to a poor, lower-class Black woman named Louise Howard. Secretly ashamed of his new wife, the young man keeps her hidden from his socially prominent, middle-class mother. Louise, who has been molested and beaten by her drunken father, meets Alvin Hilliard and spoils the plans of her father which include kidnapping her for the purpose of singing at the night club of one of his racketeer friends. During a confrontation between Louise, Alvin, and the racketeer (named Eddie) Alvin accidentally shoots Louise, scarring her beauty for life. The altercation leads to Alvin being sent to prison; Alvin escapes prison only to encounter Louise who has run off with Eddie the racketeer and becomes a cabaret singer. Alvin begins a new life with the daughter of a prominent attorney who is also caught up in the numbers game of racketeering. By chance, Alvin and Louise cross paths again. However, despite the fact they are both African American, Louise realizes she and Alvin are not well-matched socially. Disheartened over being unequally yoked, Louise commits suicide (Bogle, 107).

The Scar of Shame presents an effective picture on the color caste system and the consequences of social class divisions that exist within the Black community. The term (color caste) refers to a division of society based on differences of economic status, profession, occupation, or race.

According to Gaines, toward the end of the nineteenth century, Black society was characterized by a small group of aristocrats at the top and a small group at the bottom. Gaines asserts:

> Finally, it did not matter exactly how many blacks "were or weren't" middle class achievers because what was important was the challenge to white assumptions that blacks could not possibly be this or that.
>
> Like much of the black literary production of the day, then, race movies were thoroughly imbued with the spirit and the letter of uplift, the mode in which race consciousness was publically articulated in the early part of the twentieth century. (Gaines, 107)

Moreover, a larger issue needs to be addressed with respect to the films creation of a phantom social hierarchy in which Black society struggles to make its own illusory "middle" while economic conditions having to do with Black migration north are enlarging the lower group (4).

Jane Gaines takes a different approach toward the use of the term "melodrama" when addressing social issues within the Black community versus the earlier argument posed by Thomas Cripps. She argues that melodrama reenacts a moral pattern, which coincides with the value system in operation within a particular point in history (5). A world that is constructed by melodrama, according to Gaines, becomes a safe haven for the emotional expression of volatile issues. The ethical patterns and the distribution of remuneration and retribution in melodramas are always made to fit local assumptions and prevailing theses. Thus, the melodrama becomes an extremely acquiescent and receptive genre that accommodates the social problems of every new decade, stirring an audience in its time but never striking a cord for another generation.

Gaines places emphasis on the fact that racial uplift stories lend themselves to melodramatic treatment because the uplift philosophy, like the melodrama, is built upon a basis paradox (5). However, at a time when self-esteem issues were at the forefront of concerns amongst African Americans, why place so much emphasis on skin color? What was so uplifting about *The Scar of Shame*? As stated earlier, it was and still is a well-known fact within the Black community that the subject of hue provides grounds for a divisive discussion.[8] Moreover, class distinctions are still a cause of disagreement amongst Black Americans. Therefore, why display images on the screen that depict Blacks as racketeers, unethical, and misogynistic? Perchance the answer to this question is when the cooperative experience includes White America, (especially as it relates to the development of Black art, which in this case I am calling Black film) the purity of the art form becomes diluted, and the process of hegemony continues to divide the people. Conversely, *The Scar of Shame* raises several questions not only pertaining to the color caste system, but also the authenticity of Black film.

THE BLOOD OF JESUS: AN UPLIFTING MESSAGE
TO THE AFRICAN AMERICAN COMMUNITY

"All God's Chillun" and "Amazing Grace" were two familiar Gospel songs played on the sound track of *The Blood of Jesus* (1941). *The Blood of Jesus*, which Cripps refers to as a subgenre of Black film is a classic example of a film that not only included an all-Black cast, but also was actually written, produced, and directed by African Americans. This film, written and directed by Spencer Williams Jr. of television's *Amos 'n' Andy Show* (who also plays Ras Williams in the film), is a morality story which examines the Christian experience within an African American context. The film emerges from a Black perspective and focuses on the structure of Black southern religion. Similar to the work of Eloise Gist, the Black evangelist who traveled the South displaying her movies in various churches in the 1930s, Williams's theological concerns center on the possibility and promise of individual transformation through Christian belief in the workings of God's grace. Additionally, he places special emphasis on the reality of the divine presence in the lives of individuals, and the assurance of just punishment for those who fail to commit to a life ordered by faith (Weisenfeld, 94).

In *The Blood of Jesus*, Williams uses the cross and crossroads to represent the spiritual and social journey taken by African Americans since enslavement in America. The focus of the storyline revolves around the near death experience of Martha Jackson (Cathryn Caviness), a newly baptized woman whose new husband, Ras (Spencer Williams), refuses to have anything to do with her church. When Ras returns from hunting on the same Sunday that Martha has been baptized, his rifle falls and he accidentally shoots her in her heart. For the rest of the film Martha's spirit, which is separated from her body, attempts to find its way back, but it first must withstand various temptations that Satan (played by Jas. B. Jones) places in her path (Weisenfeld, 96). Facing death, she must choose between Hell, represented as the "city" or urban life, and Zion, represented as pastoral America, which symbolizes opportunity and freedom for "All of God's Chillun."[9] The climax comes when Martha makes her decision at the foot of the cross and wakes up to family, church community, and the singing of her church choir.

According to religion scholar Judith Weisenfeld, Spencer Williams drew on and translated African American folklore traditions and Black Christian approaches to biblical and other broad religious narratives for film (112). Furthermore, Weisenfeld states that, "The goal of the film was not necessarily to convince viewers of the literal truth of these things as embodied in the film, but to promote the moral truths that underlie the film story and iconography" (112). One controversial issue surrounds the financing of the film. It was clearly understood that with *The Scar of Shame*, the financial support was provided by White producers and distributors of Black- audience films. In question, is how much, if any, financial support was provided by White producers Alfred N. Sack and Harry M. Popkin. Whatever the case, dissimilar to *The Scar of Shame* where African Americans were left out of the decision making process, Sack was a hands off producer who allowed Williams the opportunity to express himself artistically.

Williams completed the film just before the outbreak of World War II. During the war, a shortage of raw film stock curtailed the making of Race movies, thus preventing Williams and Sack from making a sequel (Cripps, 98). *The Blood of Jesus* succeeded in the eyes of its fans evident by the support the film received from the Black press. [10]

> Blood of Jesus (film); Spencer Williams; Regal Theater; Hailed by enthusiastic audiences everywhere as "the most powerful all Negro motion picture ever produced," "The Blood of Jesus," Spencer Williams newest production, will be shown at the regal Theater for one night, beginning midnight July 31. (*Chicago Defender*, 10)

Additionally, Spencer Williams's religious themes provided a message of hope and unity within the African American Community.

THE END AND BEGINNING OF A NEW ERA

While mainstream Hollywood filmmakers demeaned the African American, an underground movement gave rise to a group of independent Black filmmakers who flourished during the late 1920s and 1930s (Bogle, 102). Early Black filmmakers such as William Foster, Oscar Micheaux, and Spencer Williams tried to present positive images and realistic portrayals of Black America. However, they were frequently afflicted by financial concerns, technical issues, problems with distribution, and controversial storylines. Oscar Micheaux's 1920 film, *Within Our Gates* sparked a controversy because of an explosive lynching sequence. The fear that it might inspire race riots caused the Chicago Board of Censors to originally reject the film. When the film finally opened in Chicago its national distribution was limited. Southern theaters refused to book it; it later disappeared (Bogle, 116). Micheaux was at the center of controversy again in 1938 when the Young Communist League boycotted his film *God's Stepchildren* (1938). The boycott, which involved picketing the RKO Theatre at the Harlem premiere, declared that the film "creates a false splitting of Negroes in to light and Dark groups" (Gaines, 126). The splitting of the races was a discriminatory practice used by White employers in Harlem. Employers would often divide workers against each other based on skin color. However, it is worth noting that the boycott was organized as a recruiting tool for Black membership by the Young Communist League. On one hand, Micheaux has been criticized for selecting light-complexion actors for prominent roles, for selecting genres of film that imitate Hollywood, and for his poor standards in technical quality. On the other hand, Donald Bogle points out that films such as *God's Step Children* reflect the racial philosophy of the Black middle classes in the 1930s and 1940s (115).

Race films made strong statements regarding class, color caste, and religion, while at the same time highlighting the conflict that exists between the distinctions of Whiteness versus Blackness. In *The Scar of Shame*, a common theme focuses on the conflict between the educated, articulate, light-skinned protagonist Alvin Hilliard, whereas Louise Howard's dark complexion becomes a symbol of inferiority. Throughout the movie, the lower-class characters had darker skin color, while those characters portrayed as intellectuals (the Black *bourgeois*), had light skin color. To stress the purity of Whiteness, special lighting was used to make the actors' skin tone even lighter. "The stylistic discourse carrying the melos is connected to the aesthetics of skin tone and hair texture played out in light, shadow, and shade. This color scheme or code would be known in its finer gradations and variations only to black audiences" (Gaines, 14). Moreover, the color scheme advocates for light skin privilege (Colorism). Colorism, which characterizes White supremacy, is a byproduct of slavery suggesting that those with lighter skin will do better economically and within society. According to Donald Bogle, "The girl's father is very dark; so, too, is the racketeer. Almost all the other characters are fair skinned. This girl is clearly a victim of her 'dark' biological background" (107). Thus, the color schemes encourage the distinction between Whiteness as beautiful (good) and Blackness as ugly (evil).

Black genre films emerge from a segregated point of view, even when addressing "White" themes; they rely on an appropriate collection of symbols (Cripps, 10). According to Cripps, symbols may include a folk idiom such as Black religion (*The Blood of Jesus*), or a cultured blues idiom (*The St. Louis Blues*) that evolved from a rhythmic celebrated Black life. "Black genre films celebrates *aesthetique du cool*, the outward detachment, composed choreographic strides, and self-posed, enigmatic mask over inner urgency that have been admired in both Africa and [Black] America" (Cripps, 12). Moreover, the *aesthetique du cool* is a celebration of triumph over adversity, fellow feelings, and moral superiority of the oppressed, which, according to Cripps, is often reflected in Black movies.

In 1929 the British journal *Close-up* devoted an entire issue to the "The negro in Film." Editor Kenneth Macpherson captured the tone of the issue in his introduction when he bemoans the demise of the silent films. Macpherson concurs with other writers that "the talkies now made it possible to hear the Negro for the first time" (Gaines, 1). According to Gaines, amid this sudden new flavor of cultural fare about film and Black American life, questions emerge from the contributors to this special British issue regarding the possibilities of a new world cinema that was inclusive of a Black voice. Gaines concludes by stating:

> "Race movies" were a magical inhabitation of white forms, deriving their power from that which Blacks were not (whites), using that power to become better. . . .
>
>   Black race movie pioneers, taking some things and leaving others, brought about change by means of a complex and imaginative incorporation, not simple assimilation. (23)

Although limited, the Black voice in film managed to survive well before 1929; I would argue that the Black filmmaker's dream for creative expression continues to be suppressed by a White hegemonic culture. In interviews with Henry Louis Gates and *Complex* magazine, Black filmmaker Spike Lee supports the statement of White hegemony in film. Lee is vocal about the fact that

> Hollywood is predominantly white. You don't see too many people of color behind the scenes. You don't. You go to any studio, the black guy you are going to see is the guy at the gate. In Hollywood, there is not one African-American who is an executive that has a gatekeeper position that could green-light a picture And you talk about apartheid; it's really the studios. They'll make a film with Denzel and Jamie and Eddie, but only because they can make money off them. But when you look at how they are staffed, there is no diversity. They might think there's diversity because four white women run studios.
>
>   We set a precedent with *She's Gotta Have It,* and ever since then [Hollywood] knew that if they were to do business with me, I would have to have full creative control. (2,179)

Thomas Cripps avows that we must recognize Black film as an inimitable case of genre film. He contends that no other genre, except perhaps the American western, spoke so directly to the meaning and importance of shared values embraced by its audience (Cripps, 12). The Black hero in race films embraces values that focus on the family structure and social meaning that have served as safeguards for Black America. Black heroes win against the system; they allow for the temporary defeat of a discriminatory social structure.

The historical significance of race films has not only added new dimensions to African American cinema, but has paved the way for a "new voice" of young independent Black filmmakers. Armed with impudent visions, filmmakers such as Charles Burnett (*To Sleep with Anger*), Tim Story (*Barbershop,* and the *Fantastic Four* movies), David E. Talbert (*First Sunday*), Matty Rich (*Straight out of Brooklyn*), and Mario Van Peebles (*New Jack City*) continue to offer an alternative voice to mainstream Hollywood.

In *The Scar of Shame,* the room where Louise dies symbolizes the life she relinquished by her compromise. The iris-out ending of books and a candle at the end of the Louise's suicide scene represent a summation of her wasted life (Cripps, 71). Perhaps Louise's suicide symbolically represents a new beginning in African American cinema as well as the death of an obscure term that has been used to denote a particular film genre called race movies.[11]

Figure 1.1.   Paul Robeson starred in the film *Body and Soul* (1925), which was directed and produced by Oscar Micheaux. His other notable film credits include *The Emperor Jones* (1933), *Show Boat* (1936), *Song of Freedom* (1936), *Big Fella* (1937), *King Solomon's Mines* (1937), *Jericho* (1937), and *Tales of Manhattan* (1942). Library of Congress, Prints & Photographs Division, Carl Van Vechten Collection, reproduction number LC-DIG-ppmsca-18633.

Figure 1.2.   Rex Ingram plays the role of "De Lawd" in the film *The Green Pastures* (1936). The film featured an all-Black cast. Library of Congress, Prints & Photographs Division, Carl Van Vechten Collection, reproduction number LC-DIG-ds-01153.

Figure 1.3. Ethel Waters plays the lead role of Petunia Jackson in the film *Cabin in the Sky* (1943). Library of Congress, Prints & Photographs Division, Carl Van Vechten Collection, reproduction number LC-USZ62-114460.

Figure 1.4. Actress/Dancer Josephine Baker. Library of Congress, Prints & Photographs Division, Carl Van Vechten Collection, reproduction number LC-DIG-ppmsca-07816.

Figure 1.5. Legendary blues singer Bessie Smith starred in the all-Black-cast short film *St. Louis Blues* (1929). Library of Congress, Prints & Photographs Division, Carl Van Vechten Collection, reproduction number LC-DIG-ppmsca-09571.

NOTES

1. Race films are also referred to as "race cinema" and "ethnic cinema" (Cook, 302).

2. The Colored Players Film Corporation, a Philadelphia-based production company, was a leading maker of race films in the late 1920s. CPFC was launched by European-American Jews: producers David Starkman, Louis Groner, and Roy Calnek. The company released four feature films between 1926 and 1929: *A Prince of His Race* (1926), *Ten Nights in a Barroom* (1926), *Children of Fate* (1927), and *The Scar of Shame* (Musser uses 1929 as the release date for this film), (Musser, 178).

3. The "New Negro" is a phrase that is also used to illustrate the migration of the urban Negro, an African American who moved from southern farms in the South to the North.

4. Everett, 9.

5. Charlene B. Regester's annotated bibliography of four major Black newspapers, lists over twelve thousand articles pertaining to Black entertainers in African American newspaper articles.

6. See appendix A.

7. Three dates are given as the release date for this film. The three dates are 1926, 1927, and 1929. According to Jane Gaines, *The Scar of Shame* was dated by scholars as 1926 and 1927 for many years, but recent research shows that it was first exhibited in 1929.

8. Spike Lee's film *Jungle Fever* crosses the Black-White border. In the wake scene, Black women are sitting around discussing the complexities surrounding the issues of different shades of Blackness.

9. Williams' later also addressed the essence of migration and urbanization of African Americans and the moral implications of the geographic shift from the South to the North.

10. Refer to Charlene B. Regester's annotated bibliography.

11. Special Note: For more information regarding the Van Vechten Collection at the Library of Congress contact the Library of Congress at: www.loc.gov/.

TWO

Riding the Train of Cultural Complexity with Sarah Jane and Clay

Critique of the Films Imitation of Life and Dutchman

The gospel train is coming, I hear it just at hand,
I hear the car wheels moving, And rumbling thro' the land.
Get on board little children, Get on board little children,
There's room for many more . . .
The fare is cheap and all can go, The rich and poor are there
No second class aboard this train, No difference in the fare.
— "De Gospel Train," by the Fisk Jubilee Singers

In the films *Imitation of Life* (1959) and *Dutchman* (1967), two intricate cultural themes are presented within the storylines.[1] In *Imitation of Life*, the character Sarah Jane rejects her racial identity and attempts to pass for White. She is obsessed with the obvious preference for Whiteness (and the privileges associated with it) that dominates our society. In Amiri Baraka's film adaptation of his play, *Dutchman*, the character Clay struggles to come to terms with his personal identity as a Black male living in the 1960s. Clay is hesitant about rejecting a value system based on a White hegemonic structure for fear it would deter his efforts towards Black integration. Similar to Sarah Jane, Clay wants to be accepted by White America. In my critique, I consider the impact and influence of White societal suppression within the Black community and how suppression diminishes the opportunity for development of an authentic "Black identity." Additionally, this chapter examines the historical and cultural influences of Black Nationalism on the Black American artist in an attempt to aesthetically define Black artistic expression. In both films, I explore the racial themes, literary texts, and how the narrative decon-

19

structs Black and White relations in America. My discussion regarding the complexities of "racial consciousness" begins with Douglas Sirk's 1959 film adaptation, *Imitation of Life*.

The historical significance associated with the definition of "who is Black" dates back to slavery and continued with the Jim Crow system. In the South, the creation of the "One Drop Rule" was critical in distinguishing racial traits from cultural traits and defining Black African ancestry in the United States. To what extent do African Americans suffer from a color complex and low self-esteem issues? The film *Imitation of Life* (which is based on the novel by Fannie Hurst) illustrates the historical and cultural implications of the term "passing" and the influence of societal suppression within the Black community. The narrative suggests that a suppressive environment diminishes the opportunity for development of an authentic "Black identity."

The formation of racial boundaries in the United States by White America created a racial hierarchy and several cultural walls of complexities within the Black community; these same walls continue to be a stumbling block for Black Americans even today. In order for Black America to continue down a progressive path toward the construct of a positive Black identity, a cry for freedom should be made, similar to the one Ronald Reagan gave in a speech to Soviet Union leader Mikhail Gorbachev at the Brandenburg Gate on June 12, 1987, regarding the destruction of the Berlin Wall. However, while Reagan was making a plea for one wall to come down across the globe, several walls representing racial prejudice, inequity, and other issues pertaining to Colorism were still erected in his own country. Moreover, the walls of discrimination in America stood long before the Berlin Wall was erected in 1961.

According to F. James Davis, "To be considered Black, not even half of one's ancestry must be African black" (4). Davis's comments are in reference to a rule that was constructed to distinguish between who was considered Black and who was considered White in America—the term "the one drop rule" dates back to colonial America. The one drop rule states that if a person had one single drop of Black blood running through their veins, they would be considered Black. Furthermore, the southern judicial systems (during and after the Reconstruction Era in particular) supported what they called "the traceable amount rule." As a result, the rules created a pernicious method by which White America could continue hegemonic suppression based on the identifiable physical feature of the African.

Definition of the One Drop Rule—A Few Points to Consider:

1. The historical significance associated with the definition of "Who is Black," dates back to slavery and continued with the Jim Crow system.

Figure 2.1.   The film *Imitation of Life* is an adaptation of Fannie Hurst's (pictured) 1933 novel. Library of Congress, Prints & Photographs Division, Carl Van Vechten Collection, reproduction number LC-DIG-ggbain-33537.

2. Am I Black because I look Black? Is Blackness determined by skin color? Do physical features play a role in identifying Blackness? Does my ancestry have anything to do with it? What are the determining factors in defining my Blackness?

3. The United States considered a person Black if they had one single drop of Black blood running through their veins. The one drop rule only applied to Black Americans. However, contrary to the "One

Drop Rule," do all light skinned Black people have "White blood" somewhere in their lineages?

The connection between skin color and social status within the African American community dates back to slavery when "the Massa" (aka "the Master") repeatedly gave his illegitimate, mixed breed children special privileges. Certain light-skinned slaves were assigned the privileged status of house servant (often referred to as House Nigger—the post mod reference today would be House Nigga) and skilled craftsperson. Bottom-line, light skinned slaves received better treatment than darker-skinned field slaves.

THE QUESTION OF SELF-ESTEEM
WITHIN THE BLACK COMMUNITY

Douglas Sirks's melodramatic attempt to create a discourse regarding the complexities of race in the film *Imitation of Life* is intriguing, considering we live in a society that regards some people as dominant or superior versus others as less significant or inferior: "Sarah Jane's been 'passin' at school . . . pretending she's white" (Annie, *Imitation of Life*, 1959). However, within the Black community the topic of lightness versus "Rightness" has been a debated issue for quite some time. According to bell hooks, "Racial integration was hotly debated in the early sixties. The issue of whether Black people were inferior to Whites and therefore would be unable to do well in an integrated work or school context was commonly discussed" (2). bell hooks also states:

> Militant antiracist political struggles placed the issue of self-esteem for black folks on the agenda. And it took the form of primarily discussing the need for positive images. The slogan "black is beautiful" was popularized in an effort to undo the negative racist iconography and representations of blackness that had been an accepted norm in visual culture. . . . Most discussions of black people and self-esteem start by identifying racism as the sole culprit. Certainly the politics of race and racism impinge on our capacity as black folk to create self-love rooted in healthy self-esteem, sometimes in an absolute and brutal manner. Yet many of us create healthy self-esteem in a world where white supremacy and racism remain the norm. (2, 21)

I would agree with hooks and suggest that historically, the construct of racial boundaries by White Americans has not only led to issues of second-class citizenship and ethnic classifications in America, but it also forced Blacks to re-classify and question who they were as a people. Reclassification led to separation—moreover, the separation because of skin tone led to the establishment of "brown bag societies" by Blacks who were considered free.

Brown bag societies (based on the brown bag theory) were an elite group of light-skinned African Americans who were afforded special privileges in society because of the complexion of their skin. During a recent interview with Joseph Kapsch from *The Warp*, Academy Award nominee Viola Davis had this to say regarding the brown bag theory:

> When you do see a woman of color onscreen, the paper-bag test is still very much alive and kicking. That's the whole racial aspect of colorism: If you are darker than a paper bag, then you are not sexy, you are not a woman, you shouldn't be in the realm of anything that men should desire. And in the history of television and even in film, I've never seen a character like Annalise Keating played by someone who looks like me. My age, my hue, my sex. She is a woman who absolutely culminates the full spectrum of humanity our askew sexuality, our askew maternal instincts. She's all of that, and she's a dark-skin black woman. (Joseph Kapsch, *The Warp*)

Arguably before the debated subject of "White privilege" made its way through the corridors of the academy, another form of ethnic favor, "Mulatto privilege," was present within our society. Does it still exist today?

Mulatto privilege (the politically correct term today for Mulatto would probably be "bi-racial") afforded light-skinned African Americans the opportunity for economic and political advances. Furthermore, Mulatto privilege also created a "Black communal hegemony" that permitted light-skinned African Americans to have a position of elitism and dominance within their own ethnic community and gave them access to education, economic resources and political power. Light-skinned African Americans were also able to secure positions among the upper and middle-class ranks within society.

"Mulatto Privilege": Does It Still Exist Today? A Few Points to Consider:

1. Mulatto privilege afforded light-skinned African Americans the opportunity for economic and political advances.
2. Mulatto privilege (which I compare to the concept of White privilege) created a "Black communal hegemony" that permitted light-skinned African Americans to have a position of elitism and dominance within their own ethnic community and gave them access to education, economic resources and political power.
3. Light-skinned African Americans were treated differently than darker-skinned African Americans. The job opportunities were much better for "light skinned" brothers and sisters. The lighter your hue, the better your chances would be to secure positions among the upper and middle-class ranks in society as well as in Hollywood.

4. Viola Davis is correct in her assessment that dark-skin actresses were often cast for demeaning character roles (drug addicts, hookers) in Hollywood.

PASSING FOR WHITE: DOES SARAH JANE REALLY HAVE A COLOR COMPLEX?

Escapism, according to Sirk, seems to be a priority for Sarah Jane in *Imitation of Life*. Douglas Sirk's description of Sarah Jane's determination to escape her Black mother and current condition not only depicts a weakness in her character, but the conflict also opens the door for social criticism. According to Marina Heung, "Sarah Jane's whiteness is crucial in dictating our view of her having a problem, that is to say, a neurosis compounded of identity confusion, a daughter's unreasonable rejection of her mother, and opportunistic exploitation of an accident of nature to defraud society" (313). Sarah Jane's distorted efforts to escape the truth of who she was led to another problematic situation for her and her White boyfriend Frankie. Frankie confronts Sarah Jane and asks her the question: "Is it true? Is your Mother a Nigger?" Sarah Jane replies: "What difference does it make?" Apparently, it made a big difference to Frankie. In the most violent scene in the film, Sarah Jane suffers the consequence for being Black in America; she is repeatedly struck in the face by Frankie. Do Frankie's repetitive open and closed fist slaps represent White America's hatred towards Blackness?

Historically, the phrase "passing for White" represents a controversial subject that focuses on African Americans demeaning each because of hue. This gradation of color created a cultural negativity that had led to serious racial sensitivity within the Black community. Sarah Jane was determined to pass over to the other side. However, the other side for Sarah Jane (played by Susan Kohner) meant identifying with one race, while denying another. Her identification with the "other" suggests the acceptance of negative iconic visual images (stereotypes) that have haunted Black Americans for so many years.

The Color Complexities of Sarah Jane: A Few Points to Consider:

1. Does escapism for Sarah Jane suggest denial of who she is?
2. Historically, the term "passing for White" represents a controversial subject that focuses on African Americans demeaning each other because of hue. This concept only applied to Blacks and originated during slavery (F. James Davis).
3. The gradation of color created a cultural negativity that has led to serious racial sensitivity within the Black community. Discussions amongst Black Americans regarding the term "high yellow"

(which referred to Blacks who are light skin) intensified during the Harlem Renaissance when African American cultural and economic expressions across urban areas were being taken more seriously. Is the term "high yellow" still relevant today? Or is it just another derogatory word that carries a lot of historical baggage?

Imitation of Life (1959) illustrates the double bind situations which often occurred between mother-daughter relationships in the 1950s (Walters). According to the double bind theory, it was not uncommon for mothers to become emotionally unresponsive and insensitive to the needs of their children. Double bind situations produced mothers that were torn between the "narratives of Popular Culture" and the struggles of everyday life (Walters). However, according to the theory, mothers had a tendency to send conflicting messages (mixed signals) which often led to apprehension and misperceptions by their children (Berry, *Psychology Today*). Furthermore, Sirk uses the concept of double bind to emphasize the various dilemmas mothers and daughters were often confronted with in society.

Imitation of Life (1959) is about mother-daughter relationships, class conflicts, and racial concerns that develop through family interactions. Annie Johnson (played by Juanita Moore) is a single, widowed Black mother befriended by a young White aspiring actress named Lora Meredith (played by Lana Turner). They meet on Coney Island during a search for Lora's daughter Susie, who was missing. The two mothers become close and Lora invites Annie and her daughter Sarah Jane to come live with her and Susie. Susie is outspoken, inquisitive, and seeks attention from her mother. On the other hand, Sarah Jane is struggling with identity issues regarding her race; she rejects the love and attention her mother tries to give her as a result.

Since she is Black, Sarah Jane spends most of the film passing as White—an act that is sinful and heartbreaking for her mother, Annie. In the meantime, Lora practically ignores her own daughter (Susie) in her quest for stardom on the Broadway stage. Lora achieves fame and fortune while Sarah Jane flees the controversial spotlight of racial separation. Both characters were fully engaged, yet, misguided in their search for acceptance, love, and true happiness; thus they made a mockery of their current relationships. Their obsessive desires for what they did not have forced them to be disappointed with what they already had obtained. Their repeated attempts to avoid conflict and not address their own personal identity issues eventually led to unhappiness and several dysfunctional relationships.

Sarah Jane's zealous efforts to "crossover" ultimately result in a final curtain call of denial with regards to her relationship with her mother, Annie:

Motel, interior, night

SARAH JANE: Doors open!

SARAH JANE: I'll be ready in a minute!

SARAH JANE: I hope they're not here.

ANNIE: Now, don't be mad, honey, nobody saw me.

Annie, fully aware of Sarah Jane's personal sensitivity to her Blackness and pursuit of White privilege, tries to soften the blow of her unexpected visit to Sarah Jane's place of employment—a cabaret show in Los Angeles:

SARAH JANE: You were there tonight! Oh why can't you just leave me alone?!

ANNIE: I tried, Sarah Jane. You'll never know how hard I tried.

SARAH JANE: Well, I might as well pack.

ANNIE: Look, baby—

SARAH JANE: I suppose you been to the boss! Lost me my job . . . my friends!

Sarah Jane is referencing a prior event that occurred with her former employer Harry's Club—a seedy gentlemen's club in New York. Sarah Jane had lied to Annie about her employment (she told Annie she was working the night shift at a library). As a result of Annie's appearance at Harry's Club and identification that she was Sarah Jane's (Black) mother, the club terminated Sarah Jane's employment (thus the line, "I suppose you been to the boss! Lost me my job . . . my friends!")

ANNIE: I've been no place! I didn't come to bother you—

SARAH JANE: Well, you won't. Not ever again. Spoil things for me here and I'll just go somewhere else.

SARAH JANE: I'll keep on going until you are so tired and so . . .

ANNIE: Baby—I am tired. I am as tired as I ever want to be. You mind if I sit down?

SARAH JANE: Yes, I do. Somebody's coming. That's why the door was unlocked.

ANNIE: I'll only stay a minute. I just want to look at you. That's why I came. Are you happy here, honey? Are you findin' what you really want?

SARAH JANE: I'm somebody else! I'm white! White! WHITE! Does that answer you?

ANNIE: I guess so.

According to Marina Heung, "Sarah Jane's refusal to accept her racial identity leads her to reject her mother and, indirectly, to cause her mother's death" (312). Sarah Jane's rejection of who she was ultimately led to her separation of identity. Sadly, Sarah Jane failed to recognize that Annie's statement "Baby—I am tired. I am as tired as I ever want to be" was a comment directed toward the plight of African Americans in the United States. A similar statement was made by Rosa Parks on December 1, 1955, in Montgomery, Alabama, when she refused to give up her seat in the colored section to a White passenger. When asked by the bus driver: "Are you going to stand up?" Rosa Parks replied: "No." Rosa Parks got on the bus first and paid the same fare as everyone else—why stand up so that a White man (who got on later) could sit down? (Theoharis, 63). Annie (akin to Rosa) was tired of disparity—however, she accepted the fact that God made her Black; like Rosa, Annie was determined and not ashamed of who she was.

In her novel *Imitation of Life* (1933), Fannie Hurst's principle character Delilah (which is the character Annie Johnson in Sirk's 1959 film adaptation) suggests that cheating on color is a refusal to accept distinctiveness as a human being based on how God created you. In essence, the refusal to accept how you were made by God may not go over too well with "de Lawd":

> Cheatin' on color jes' because de Lawd left out a little drop of black dye in de skin that dat covers up her black blood. How kin I get mah baby out of her crucifyn' herself over de color of de blood de Lawd seen fit in His wisdom to give her . . . She can't pass. Nobody cain't pass. God's watchin'. God's watchin' for to cotch her. (225)

From the novel, Delilah considers her daughter's attempt to pass for White to be sinful: "Lawd help her and Lawd help me to save her sinning little soul" (226). Equally, in the film adaptation Annie delivers a similar line stating: "It is a sin to be ashamed of what you are, even worse to pretend." However Peola (which is the character Sarah Jane in the 1959 film adaptation) disagrees. For Peola (and Sarah Jane), the real sin was being forced to accept an identity or situation that was counterproductive to the construct of who they really wanted to be. Perhaps the debate was never about denial, for denial helps a person avoid a potentially disturbing fact. Nevertheless, acceptance of the truth sometimes requires that you do all you can to deal with a given situation.

Through the lens of a camera, Douglas Sirk artistically paints a picture of numerous disturbing facts and an American social consciousness that many would not dare touch in 1959. Yet, in his attempt to bury Annie during the last scene, the funeral (the general consensus from critics of the film is that Annie's death was caused by a broken heart), does Sirk also resurrect issues that have plagued this country and African Americans for many years concerning low self-esteem, Colorism (which is the practice of discrimination and showing favor based on lighter skin versus darker skin) and a negative Black identity? Or was Sirk (and producer Ross Hunter) trying to bury a subject that most White Americans are uncomfortable discussing—the racial divide in America. Maybe so . . . maybe both.

> Then they spat in his face and struck him with their fists. And some slapped him, saying, "Prophesy for us, you Christ! Who hit you?"
> —Matthew 26:67 (*Net Bible*)

TRAGICALLY SPEAKING, WHAT IS BLACK ART? AFFIRMING A BLACK AESTHETIC IN THE BLACK ARTS MOVEMENT

The Black Arts Movement was a compelling time in America as many Black artists were posing questions concerning issues of authenticity, creativity, and personal agency during the Movement's early formation in the 1960s. As opposed to the Harlem Renaissance and referred to as the artistic Sister to the Black Power Movement, the ideological foundation for the Black Arts Movement was its conviction for Black unity and its connection to Black Nationalism.[2]

The shift by some Black thinkers towards a more mainstream approach to the presentation of Black literature and political protest proved to be problematic. As Black intellectual thought continued to develop during the 1960s and 1970s, Black intellectuals and artists desegregated from the very communities of Blackness that produced them. For these early pioneers of the Black Arts Movement, the preservation of Black expression was an obvious concern and crucial to the development of a new Black aesthetic. On the other hand, the question left unanswered is does one preserve Black expression within a White hegemonic society that has pre-set the standards for cultural values and artistic beauty?

Considered the pioneer of the Black Arts Movement, playwright Amiri Baraka successfully used drama as an effective interactive tool for Black expression. Baraka's arduous efforts in the development of Propaganda Theater during the 1960s, created a venue for the Black artist and established an independent voice within the Black community.[3] Moreover,

Figure 2.2.   The great gospel singer Mahalia Jackson plays the role of a choir soloist singing the song "Trouble of the World" in the film *Imitation of Life* (1959). Library of Congress, Prints & Photographs Division, Carl Van Vechten Collection, reproduction number LC-US262-91314.

Baraka's 1964 play *Dutchman* explored in dramatic parable the aesthetic of political and social alienation faced by Black America during the 1960s.

Dutchman, a one-act play, was first staged at the Cherry Lane Theatre in New York City in 1964. A winner of the Obie Award for best off-Broadway play, Baraka turned his talents to the silver screen, adapting his play to film in 1967. *Dutchman* is a transitional piece that pivots from Baraka's earlier non-conformist poetic/stage work to his revolutionary views pertaining to his advocacy for racial equality, Black separatism, and Black Nationalism. Much of Baraka's later work focused on subjects pertaining to Black awareness, Black liberation, and racism.

Dutchman, which is a powerful illustration of the problems of Black identity in White culture, alludes to the legendary Flying Dutchman, a ship of dead sailors said to haunt the high seas. The legend of the Flying Dutchman, which gained popularity through the operatic work of Richard Wagner in 1843, presents a story of a ship's captain condemned to sail until Judgment Day. The setting for the plot of *Dutchman* presents a similar scenario by symbolically linking the main characters to the Flying Dutchman legend: Clay (the main character) who represents the God figure; and Lula (the other main character) as the captain (Hatch and Shine, 381). It is from this linkage the two main characters ride a "subway train on a continuous journey in the flying underbelly of the city New York" (382).

The characters in Dutchman are presented to the audience as follows: CLAY, a twenty-year-old Negro whose characteristics include critical reason, self-control, perfection, the dream state, illusion of human beings as artists, and exhaustion of possibilities; LULA, a thirty-year-old White woman whose characteristics include intoxication, celebration of nature, glorification of art, and destruction; RIDERS OF THE COACH (who are White and Black); a YOUNG NEGRO and CONDUCTOR.[3] To Clay, Lula is a White beauty; to Lula, Clay is a member of the Black bourgeoisie, determined to achieve success at any expense and willing to sell his soul on the conditions established by a White American capitalistic system.

What are the terms for achieving artistic success in White America? Nita Kumar's analysis of *Dutchman* illustrates the essence of societal conflicts between a "White aesthetic" and a "Black aesthetic" in White America. In her essay, Kumar describes Lula's character as aggressive, enticing and insulting (275). Moreover, Lula's abrasive, White supremacist nature is apparent as she refers to Clay as "a liver-lipped white man, just a dirty white man." Her abrasive dialogue continues:

> **LULA**: Screw yourself, Uncle Tom. Thomas Woolly-Head. There is Uncle Tom. I mean, Uncle Thomas Woolly-Head. With old white matted mane. He hobbles on his wooden cane. Old Tom. Old Tom. Let the white man hump his ole mama, and he jes' shuffle off in the woods and hide his gentle gray head. Ole Thomas Woolly-Head. (*Dutchman*, 1967)

Lula ends her repressive rant with: "You let me go you Black Son of Bitch." The heated exchange of words results in Clay slapping Lula and bursting into a long, dramatic monologue regarding the tortured and conflicted psyche of a Black male in America. The continual denial (or rejection) of a Black identity within any given art form by White America suppresses the opportunity for further development of a Black aesthetic, a dream that existed not only for Clay but also within the psyche of the Black man. Moreover, White societal suppression (hegemony) of Black expression diminishes optimism for a Black aesthetic and ultimately questions the realism of a so-called "Black dream."

Problematic to the discourse of a Black aesthetic is the conflict that exists between the distinctions of Whiteness versus Blackness aesthetically. What is considered good? What is considered bad? According to

Western ideology a central characteristic of the "White aesthetic" is the dichotomy of superiority versus inferiority. Early in the literature of the Middle Ages (especially in the morality plays of England), a distinction between Whiteness as beautiful (good) and Blackness as ugly (evil) was present (Gayle, 41). Heavily influenced by Platonism, the characters and plot of these plays followed a basic structure: the villain is always evil, and in most cases is the devil or the antagonist. The hero is always good, and in most cases, an angel or disciple (Gayle, 41). Thus, the distinction of Whiteness as pure, beautiful, and complete, versus the obscurity and ugliness of Blackness, reinforces the attention given to the preservation and affirmation of a Black aesthetic during the Black Arts Movement.

Amiri Baraka speaks poetically through his character Clay regarding the realness of a genuine Black identity. Aesthetically, the beauty of Blackness in the eyes of Clay is displayed through pure emotion and feelings. Moreover, for Baraka, the issue of authenticity is essential to the survival of Black Art, and is a critical element confined within the context of Clay's closing monologue:

> **CLAY**: I'll rip your lousy breasts off! Let me be who I feel like being. Uncle Tom. Thomas. Whoever. It's none of your business. You don't know anything except what's there for you to see. An act. Lies. Device. Not the pure heart, the pumping black heart. You don't ever know that. . . .

Clay's cry for freedom at the beginning of the monologue traces the connection between "Black rage" and "Black Art" but his cry ultimately results in his death:

> **CLAY**: Charlie Parker? Charlie Parker. All the hip white boys scream for Bird. And Bird saying, Up your ass, feeble-minded ofay! Up your ass. And they sit there talking about the tortured genius of Charlie Parker. Bird would've played not a note of music if he just walked up to East Sixty-Seventh Street and killed the first ten white people he saw. . . . If Bessie Smith had killed some white people she wouldn't have needed that music. (*Dutchman*, 1967)

Lula silences Clay's voice when she says, "I've heard enough," and stabs him in the chest with her knife. Additionally, the camera lens also captures the silence of the riders on the subway, who break their stillness when they are instructed by Lula to remove Clay's dead body from her lap and throw him off the train. The riders are also given directives from Lula to "get off at the next stop." The train stops and all the riders exit leaving Lulu alone in the coach until she meets another young Negro who enters and sits a few seats behind her. Lula looks up, they make eye contact, and an old Negro conductor walks by the young Negro man and greets him with the words "Hey Brother." Unaware of his cultural hegemonic surroundings, the young man responds back by saying, "Hey."

Is the tragedy in *Dutchman* really about the death of Clay or the termination of Black artistic freedom that started during the Harlem Renaissance and continued through the Black Arts Movement? *Dutchman* avows as well as denies the legitimacy of Black Art in the process of self-preservation. Furthermore, resistance by Blacks to attacks made on Black culture by a White hegemonic culture will ultimately lead to the extinction of any Black artistic expression. In the film, Baraka questions the co-existence of a White and Black aesthetic and suggests separation as an alternative. When Lula openly criticizes Clay for his pretentious White man appearance, the riders on the train are silent. Moreover, when Clay angrily expresses himself to Lula, Baraka suggests there are restraints (evident by the restraints placed on Clay by the riders on the train from attacking Lula) placed on any criticism of White culture, especially by a Black male artist.

What are the consequences for authentic freedom? What is really at stake when the Black artist ultimately defines his identity? bell hooks asserts:

> Racial integration in a social context where white supremacist systems are intact undermines marginal spaces of resistance by promoting the assumption that social equality can be attained without changes in the culture's attitudes about blackness and black people . . . .
>
> A culture of domination demands of all its citizens self-negation. The more marginalized, the more intense the demand. Since black people, especially the underclass, are bombarded by messages that have no value, are worthless, it is no wonder that we fall prey to nihilistic despair or forms of addiction that provide momentary escape, illusions of grandeur, and temporary freedom from the pain of facing reality. (10, 19)

The aesthetic illusion is critical to the development of the poetic voice. However, at what point, does the illusionary image of racial harmony and free Black artistic expression portrayed by pretentious societal beliefs, become a reality? Perhaps the answer to the former question is that the illusion will always mimic the dream. The dream for the Black artist is an opportunity to explore the freedom of creative expression. If the answer to this question is indeed artistic self-expression and self-liberation, then the death of Clay was also the affirmation of a new Black aesthetic.

Be thou faithful unto death, and I will give thee a crown of life.
—Revelations 2:10 (*KJV*)

NOTES

1. The term "Negro," which is used throughout this chapter, carries a lot of histori-cal baggage within the play and film *Dutchman*. The term was used by the Spanish and Portuguese to refer to people of African heritage. Ironically, with respect to individual identity, older African Americans (demographically 65+) have a positive identification with the term regarding their personal definition of what Blackness means to them. African Americans (which include my parents) have a strong affinity to the historical meaning of the term. Those born before the post–World War II baby boom frequently use it.

2. The Harlem Renaissance covered a period from 1920 to 1940. The creative works and essays of writers/scholars W. E. B. Du Bois, Langston Hughes, Zora Neale Hurs-ton, and Richard Wright were produced during this time. Participants in the Black Arts Movement often belittled those involved in the Harlem Renaissance for what they considered to be a disconnection with African American people. In 1971, BAM participant Haki Madhubuti states in his essay "Renaissance I To Renaissance III? An Introduction": "[T]he black arts movement in the twenties was of a minimal influ-ence . . . more whites knew about what was happening than brothers and sisters" (Collins and Crawford, 13).

3. During the 1960s, playwright/poet Leroi Jones changed his name to Amiri Bara-ka. Baraka became involved with the Black Nationalist Movement and considered himself a Black cultural nationalist. His involvement with the movement led to a divorce from his Jewish wife and separation from his two children. In 1974, Baraka distanced himself from Black Nationalism to become a Marxist and a supporter of anti-imperialist third world liberation movements. Baraka has been a subject of con-troversy regarding his poetic and dramatic works. He has been accused of writing anti-Semitic poems and articles.

THREE

Black "Zombies/Non-Zombies" that Live Amongst the Dead

A Closer Look at the Screen Acting Work of Mantan Moreland and Duane Jones in King of the Zombies *(1941) and* Night of the Living Dead *(1968)*

From frightened manservant to unsung hero, Mantan Moreland and Duane Jones were considered inspirations for their roles in two cult films: *King of the Zombies* (1941) and *Night of the Living Dead* (1968). This chapter will take a closer look at the cinematic acting performances of Mantan Moreland (as Jeff) in one of the earliest versions of the Zombie film genre, *King of the Zombies*, and Duane Jones (as Ben) in George A. Romero's *Night of the Living Dead*. Additionally, it is important to note that Romero's *Night of the Living Dead* is considered to be the catalyst for the modern day horror film. Moreover, his controversial selection of Duane Jones as Ben represented the first time an African American was cast in a starring role in a mainstream horror film. This chapter will consider the storylines and roles for both actors as well as the social commentary underscored in each film.

KING OF THE ZOMBIES, MANTAN MORELAND

During World War II an airplane which is low on fuel crashes on what appears to be a deserted island in the Caribbean. The aircraft was blown off course by a storm. There are three passengers on board: a pilot named James "Mac" McCarthy (played by Dick Purcell) another passenger, Bill

Summers (played by John Archer) and a manservant named Jefferson "Jeff" Jackson (played by the African American comedic actor Mantan Moreland). The pilot follows the guidance of transmitted radio signals he hears from the cockpit; however, the plane ultimately crashes on an island. According to Mac, they are somewhere between Cuba and Puerto Rico. This setting places all three men in a precarious situation. After the plane crashes, we find Jeff lying on the ground in front of a tombstone with the inscription, "Rest in Peace." Jeff, realizing where he is says: "Rest in peace? If that means what I think it means they sho don't waste no time around here." Moreland then delivers his signature line, which he has done in so many other films (particularly the *Charlie Chan* movies), "Let me outta here." The camera focuses on Moreland's physical ability to make his eyes bulge (and bug out), a common physical attribute of his when forced into a tense, scary situation; the audience continues to hear the line "Let me outta here" again and again.

The sound of the drum beats coming from the secluded island serves as a transitional moment for the men. Their circumstances look unwelcoming until they find what appears to be a safe haven not too far from where their plane landed. Their journey from the plane wreckage leads them to the front door of a mansion occupied by a distinguished, yet eerie looking gentleman. The observant Jeff is skeptical about who this man is and what he represents to the point of becoming terrified about their unfortunate surroundings. He soon becomes convinced the mansion is preoccupied by zombies and continues to explore his theory with the employees at the complex. Searching for any clues that could answer some questions regarding their current situation, the three men stumble upon a voodoo ritual being conducted in the cellar by the person who greeted them at the front door (audience members find out at this point the eerie looking man is a doctor). As the storyline develops, the audience also learns that the doctor (Dr. Sangre) is really a foreign spy, trying to acquire war intelligence from a captured U.S. admiral (Wainwright) whose aircraft had crashed in a similar mode on the island. While the mad scientist, Dr. Sangre, uses voodoo and hypnotism to uncover key military secrets, manservant Jeff is forced to stay in the servants' quarters with the rest of the Black zombies.

Born in Monroe, Louisiana, in 1902, Mantan Moreland began his acting career early. Reportedly, Moreland ran away from home several times to join the circus. It was during his many run away attempts that he began to develop and sharpen his comedic skills. By the late 1920s, Moreland began making the rounds through "The Chitlin' Circuit," performing on Broadway and touring Europe. At the outset, Moreland appeared in low-budget "race movies" aimed at African American audiences, but as his comedic talents came to be recognized, he received roles in larger productions—his career began to flourish during the 1940s and 1950s. Moreland is best known for his role as Birmingham Brown in the *Charlie*

Chan movies. However, it was his role as Jeff in *King of the Zombies* (considered to be a cult classic) that ultimately led to this being his signature film.

However, Moreland was often cast in roles as a buffoon, which became problematic. Over and over again he was referred to as "the man with the fastest eyes in the West" (Bogle, 72). Furthermore, Donald Bogle states that "sometimes Moreland's small stature elevated him from mere coon to a symbol of the universal little man" (74).

Moreover, the discourse that surrounds the subject of the "Coon" (a term that dates back to slavery and became popular during the minstrel shows) lends itself to other characterizations and stereotypical constructs of Black Americans by White America (e.g., "Zip Coon" or "Urban Coon," "Uncle Tom," "Magical Negro," and the "Other").

The term "zombie" is a byproduct of the Haitian religion known as Vodou. Oddly, or perhaps purposely, the Black zombies in *King of the Zombies* are practicing "Voodoo," not Vodou. Vodou (not to be confused with the religious practice of Voodoo in Louisiana) is a Haitian Creole word which originated in the Caribbean by descendents of various African groups who were enslaved and brought to a French colony on

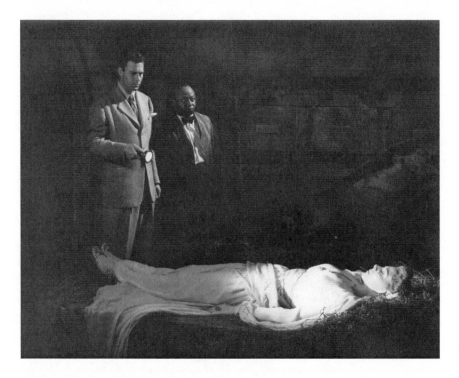

Figure 3.1. **Mantan Moreland as Jefferson "Jeff" Jackson in *King of the Zombies* (1941). Photograph from Monogram Pictures.**

the Caribbean island called Saint-Domingue (now known as Haiti). Saint-Domingue was controlled by the French on the island of Hispaniola (1625–1804) and had the largest number of enslaved Africans in the Caribbean. The main ethics of Vodou include philosophy, medicine, justice, and religion. Additionally, the fundamental principles of Vodou focus on the spiritual being. Simply stated, humans are spirits who inhabit the visible planet. According to Elizabeth McAlister, Professor of Religion at Wesleyan University:

> Vodou, a traditional Afro-Haitian religion, is a worldview encompassing philosophy, medicine, justice, and religion. Its fundamental principle is that everything is spirit. Humans are spirits who inhabit the visible world. The unseen world is populated by lwa spirits), mystè (mysteries), anvizib (the invisibles), zanj (angels), and the spirits of ancestors and the recently deceased. All these spirits are believed to live in a mythic land called Ginen, a cosmic "Africa." The God of the Christian Bible is understood to be the creator of both the universe and the spirits; the spirits were made by God to help him govern humanity and the natural world.
>
> The primary goal and activity of Vodou is to sevi lwa ("serve the spirits")—to offer prayers and perform various devotional rites directed at God and particular spirits in return for health, protection, and favour. Spirit possession plays an important role in Afro-Haitian religion, as it does in many other world religions. During religious rites, believers sometimes enter a trancelike state in which the devotee may eat and drink, perform stylized dances, give supernaturally inspired advice to people, or perform medical cures or special physical feats; these acts exhibit the incarnate presence of the lwa within the entranced devotee. Vodou ritual activity (e.g., prayer, song, dance, and gesture) is aimed at refining and restoring balance and energy in relationships between people and between people and the spirits of the unseen world. (McAlister)

Huffington Post religious journalist Antonia Blumberg has this to say about the myths of Vodou:

> On trips to New Orleans, many Americans have encountered a set of secularized traditions known as Voodoo. New Orleans Voodoo is related to but separate from Haitian Vodou. In Haiti, Vodou is an active, living religion practiced by millions of people, and a source of national identity and pride. The Haitian Creole word Vodou comes from Vodun, a word from the Fon language of modern-day Benin, meaning mysterious invisible powers that intervene in human affairs.
>
> Haitian Vodou keeps alive the theology and spiritual practices of West African cultures. Africans first came to Haiti as slaves in the sixteenth century. Their deeply rooted beliefs combined with those of Indigenous peoples already living in the Caribbean, and also combined with elements of Christianity. Because Vodou helped galvanize slaves to revolt at the end of the eighteenth century, Vodou is inextricably tied

up with Haiti's history of abolition and its establishment of an independent nation. (Blumberg)

Thus, the stereotypes of African Americans pertain to not only derogatory images of coons, Uncle Toms, and illiterate imbeciles, but also to the deconstruction and inauthenticity of sacred, cultural religious practices and images.

Conversely, another point of interest in King of the Zombies is the line delivered by the pilot Mac before the plane crashes. Mac says, "We are somewhere between Cuba and Puerto Rico." The line is not only a reference to their location geographically (which I would suggest is somewhere close to Haiti), but also draws a connection to the president of Haiti at the time, Élie Lescot. The line draws attention to and raises questions regarding the relationship and political ideologies of Haiti and the United States at the beginning of World War II.

Élie Lescot, who was biracial, had strong economic and political ties to the United States. Considered to be a repressive leader, Lescot was a member of the light-skinned "elite." The light-skinned elite were a divisive sect who focused on separating the people based on class and color. Lescot felt strongly that light skinned exclusives should be in charge and in control of all governmental matters pertaining to Haiti. Furthermore, he took control over all the state affairs by naming himself Commander in Chief and appointing a faction of light-skinned members of the elite to key posts within the régime; some of the appointees included his own sons. This action was unpopular among Haiti's mostly Black populace.

Within the context of the film King of the Zombies, the controlled zombies are deceased Black individuals. The exception is the Caucasian pilot Mac who becomes zombatized, or as Jeff calls him, a "Zumbee"; zombie is also referred to as zumbie in the Black vernacular. The deceased are revived, or brought back to life. Several of the zombies that appear to be the aggressors (especially the ones that are given directives by the leader) are fairly dark skinned African Americans. Their actions and movements are governed by a person who practices talking to the spirits of dead people and uses their magical powers for evil purposes (a necromancer); in this case, it is the doctor who is also the antagonist in the film. The zombies have no desire to function and will only respond to the commands of their leader. They remain in a "zombie-like" state; what I would argue is more of a hegemonic state of mind. Zombies are generally understood as beings trapped in an indeterminate state between life and death. Other zombie films that gave a false read and stereotype the Haitian Vodou practices are White Zombie (1932), Revolt of the Zombies (1936), and I Walked with a Zombie (1943).

It's of particular interest that the Black zombies in King of the Zombies (they were people put under the spell of voodoo and mystic traditions) were different from the flesh-eating zombies we see in Night of the Living

Dead. In *King of the Zombies*, the true horror is not being killed by zombies (which is the case in *Night of the Living Dead*), but of becoming a zombie. The older zombie films share a similar trope in their depiction of Vodou and Haitian culture as generally dangerous, menacing, and superstitious. Scholars of religious practices are quick to note that the narratives contained in the earlier zombie movies from 1930 to 1950 are subtle, and were used to construct stereotypes of Haitian and African American culture. Similar to the storylines of the Jungle genre movies during the 1940s and 1950s that featured Buster Crab in the character role of Tarzan, the story lines in these films featured false images of African Americans and depict them as rebellious savages that could only be controlled by a tree flying White man. The negative portrayals were done largely in part to satisfy White movie goers. Unfortunately for Mantan Moreland, his characters (in almost all his appearances) contributed to many of the early Black stereotypes in film.

DUANE JONES, *NIGHT OF THE LIVING DEAD*

During the early 1960s the lens through which Americans viewed images of Black Americans had changed compared to the 1940s. Racial stereotypes of buffoonery, laziness, mammies and coons were replaced by television images of protesters and supporters for civil rights, carrying signs that displayed the words "I am a Man" and "Union Justice Now." America saw the word "Vote" painted on the foreheads of protesters. America saw images of men such as Congressman John Lewis beaten after marchers in Selma, Alabama were given a two-minute warning by State Troopers to disband. Lewis states, "We just asked for two minutes so we could pray." In 1968 the assignations of Dr. Martin Luther King Jr. and Senator Robert Kennedy were challenging events in many ways for Black Americans. Dr. King, considered by many to be "The Black Moses" was snuffed out with a bullet in Memphis on April 4. Another prominent voice on behalf of the Black community, Robert Kennedy, was silenced by a bullet over June 4 and 5. The tragic assassinations of both King and Kennedy added another level of discomfort for Americans regarding race relations in 1968.

According to author Jules Witcover, "Dr. Martin Luther King Jr. the most prominent and influential civil rights leader of the era, had begun by this time to speak out forcefully against the Vietnam War as well as racial injustice at home" (5). Witcover goes on to state that King's efforts to call attention to the issues of war and the battle for equity at home were not only timely, but necessary. The country needed to hear a word regarding efforts to bring peace across the globe (by ending the war) as well as at home. Witcover continues his assessment of the current unrestrained conditions in the United States, asserting that:

Hand in hand with the war protest were racial tensions generated by joblessness and squalid living conditions in the inner cities. . . . The marriage of antiwar activists and black rights advocates was a stormy one from the start. [Stokely] Carmichael, who was a militant new voice for black power on the American left, echoed King's words at a Black Power Conference in Newark from which white reporters were barred, only days after the riots had ravaged that city. But several resolutions were adopted calling for an independent course for blacks in the country. (3)

America witnessed the bloodied beating of a man by police in Harlem on the night of Dr. King's assassination. Black America lost a champion on April, 4 1968. But perhaps they gained another one in the character Ben from *Night of the Living Dead* (1968).

In many ways, George A. Romero's *Night of the Living Dead* (1968) was a daybreak (or night of living opportunities) for Black actors in non-ethnic roles. A film filled with graphic images, satirical messages and social commentary, *Night of the Living Dead* has proven to be more than just a horror film that focuses on a group of people hiding inside a farm-house from the attack of flesh eating zombies. The protagonist in the film is the character Ben, played by African American actor Duane Jones. Originally, Ben was written to be depicted as an uncultured, unsophisticated truck driver who uses foul language. The role was intended for White actor and writer Rudy Ricci; however, Duane Jones' audition changed the mind of director Romero. According to Romero: "He simply gave the best audition" (Jones, 118).

Duane Jones was born on February 2, 1936, in New York City, New York. His academic and theatrical accomplishments included serving as the head of the Literature Department at Antioch College (1972–1976). He also taught literature at Long Island University, was the director of the Maguire Theater at the State University College at Old Westbury, and was artistic director at the Richard Allen Center for Culture and Art in Manhattan. Jones was also the executive director of the Black Theater Alliance, a federation of theater companies, from 1976 to 1981. His acting stage credits include the Negro Ensemble Company, the Actors Play-house, and the National Black Theater. Besides *Night of the Living Dead*, Jones is known for his acting work in television and roles in such films as *Ganja and Hess*, *Beat Street*, and *Losing Ground* (C. Gerald Fraserny, *NY Times.com*). Regardless of race, the talented Jones changed the mind of Romero convincing him that he was the right man for the role. Moreover, the controversial casting of Duane Jones as Ben changed the future direction in which Black actors would be cast for films.

The audience is first introduced to Ben as he flees from his truck in search of gas. He makes his way to the front porch of what appears to be an old abandoned farm house. The exact location is unknown, however, television news reports about the zombie situation (experience) indicate that the house is located in a rural area (close to Pittsburgh) in Pennsylvania. Ben is greeted at the door by an attractive blonde named Barbara who manages to make her way to the farm house after she and her brother were attacked at a cemetery while visiting the grave of their father. Barbara survived the attack, but her brother was murdered by one of the zombies. Frightened and confused, Barbara is blinded by the lights from Ben's truck, although she is still able to make contact with him. Barbara's despairing posture on the steps suggests she questions whether Ben is one of the zombies or is also trapped in what appears to be a hopeless situation.

The controversial casting of Duane Jones as Ben was just a sampling of the many challenges and controversies surrounding the American people in 1968 (refer to appendix B for a breakdown of several events from 1968 that changed the direction of how we view racism in this country). George Romero uses a strong Black male character to debunk the challenges of the stereotypical images frequently associated with Black male characters in cinema. Given his own ethnic background (Cuban) and his affinity toward the Civil Rights Movement, I would argue that the storyline of *Night of the Living Dead* is a social commentary for identity issues and civil rights for African Americans. Romero's representation of race (although race is never mentioned by any of the characters) suggest his willingness to speak to issues of discrimination, the Vietnam War, and a multiethnic society.

Ben often struggles with the personal agendas of the other occupants held captive in the farmhouse on how to survive their confinement. Furthermore, he struggles with Harry's toxic energy (we also sense that Harry possesses a bit of bigotry) which ultimately leads to a confrontation that results in Ben killing Harry. Additionally, one of the most controversial scenes is toward the beginning of the film, when Ben is forced to silence Barbara's panic attacks by punching her in the face. Barbara, who is silent for the most part up to this point, begins to open up about the loss of her brother. In her mind, "Johnny is still out there." She begins by telling Ben about what happened at the cemetery when she and her brother went to put a wreath on their father's grave. However, Romero grabs the audience's attention when we see Barbara loosen up, somewhat erotically, as she begins to tell her story. As she continues her narrative she comments: "Oh, it's hot in here . . . hot." Barbara's panic attacks (at times, they appear to be sexual in nature) are reminiscent of Leticia Musgrove's (played by Halle Berry) in the film *Monster's Ball* (2001). In the scene that probably won the Academy Award for Berry, Leticia delivers the line: "Make me feel good. I want you to make me feel good. Can you make me feel good?" However, dissimilar to Leticia, Barbara's feel good moments to free herself from personal anxiety inside the farmhouse results in her slapping Ben across the face. Ben returns the courtesy by punching her; a controversial blow considering the time period.

Critics have debated whether the character Ben was really a hero in *Night of the Living Dead*. Romero has stated Ben was just an average guy, a truck driver who (like the other occupants in the farmhouse) was trapped in what appeared to be a hopeless situation. Antonio Gramsci's concept of hegemony is apparent in *Night of the Living Dead* considering that the White Zombies metaphorically represent White America's resistance to a complex, ever changing, multicultural landscape. In the film, the White Zombies are depicted as forceful, flesh-eating creatures. Although the other dwellers in the farmhouse (who are all White) were participants in the efforts to defeat the Zombies, their contributions to make a difference were weak, which ultimately led to their demise. Moreover, at the beginning of the film and even at the end, Romero presents images of Whiteness as the dominant power.

What do people gain from going to the cinema, and how does this experience interact with their other projects, hopes, understandings, and identities? (Maltby, 14). The question references an argument concerning what people do with their cinematic experiences, and what common elements can be identified within the diversity of audience response. Scholar Richard Maltby suggests viewers demonstrate a range of modalities of responses, which vary according to their degree of personal and emotional involvement with the film and also according to their perception of its realism (14). "Historical spectators—unlike theoretical constructs—were influenced in their viewing habits by their own social and cultural identities" (17). Audience members create meanings from films based on their class, race, gender, ethnicity, religion, and political views. For many moviegoers, the character Ben in *Night of the Living Dead*, not only represented a different type of reality and unconventional identity, but he also offered a much needed theoretical framework for questioning the issues of Whiteness in other areas of social and cultural environments known as cultural inquiry.

Ben wasn't principally a hero, however; similar to so many Black Americans he became caught up in the challenges of discrimination, self-esteem issues, and survival. According to author Joe Cane:

> Many audiences perceived the parallel between America's increasingly violent civil rights struggles—particularly the then-recent assassination of Martin Luther King by racist hitman James Earl Ray, with the suspected cooperation of the FBI—and Ben's execution at the guns of the redneck posse at film's end. Without a black actor in the lead, "Night" would still have been an innovative shocker but wouldn't have hit the cultural nerves it did. (37)

In the last scene, at daybreak, Ben rises from the cellar of the farmhouse in response to the police sirens he hears. At first, Ben's rise to the top of the stairs appears to symbolize a sanguine outlook towards the positive efforts made during the Civil Rights Movement. Unfortunately for Ben and for many African Americans, his mountaintop experience ended. While looking out a window of false hope, Ben was greeted with a bullet to the forehand. The last scene in the film are a series of still shots that show men from an all-White posse standing over Ben; the imagery is similar to an angry White mob preparing for a lynching. Ben really never had a chance. Struggles against racism, oppression, poverty, police brutality, employment opportunities and economic equality were issues at the forefront of the Civil Rights Movement in 1968. Sounds like a familiar storyline for so many Black Americans in the twenty-first century.

> Who are you afraid of? I don't know why you lied to Me about it; You never seemed to care what I thought. Maybe I've been patient and quiet too long—Is that why you've lost all respect for Me? I will tell the story of your righteousness and good deeds, but they can't help you now.
>
> —Isaiah 57:1–12 (*The Voice*)

Figure 3.2.   Duane Jones as Ben in *Night of the Living Dead* (1968). Photograph from Image Ten Production.

FOUR

The Devil Made Me Do It . . .
That Is, Burn Down Paris

*Queering Masculinity in African American
Culture, American Cinema, and Television*

FLIP, DID THE DEVIL REALLY MAKE YOU DO IT?

As the Civil Rights Movement ended during the 1970s, a decline in news stories on television sets regarding anti-war demonstrations and issues of Black Nationalism also diminished. Projected on television screens across America was a message of a new beginning and a new era, especially for the African American comedian. The new Black comedian of the 1970s was strikingly different from the old school television humorists from the 1960s such as Bill Cosby and Diahann Carroll. "No longer were black stars cast as assimilated, middle-class achievers offering as many moral lessons" (MacDonald 176). According to J. Fred MacDonald, it now became intensely amusing to joke about skin color, hair texture, race riots, poverty, welfare checks, and minority social customs that also included issues of gender (177). This new wave of Black hilarity on television was provocative, emasculate, and produced a character who was the inspiration behind the popular culture phrase "What you see is what you get." The character's name, Geraldine Jones.

The *Flip Wilson Show*, a program that featured the versatile and engaging talent of Flip Wilson, appeared weekly on NBC at 8:00 pm on Thursday nights from 1970 to 1974. The show was ground-breaking in that it played host to a variety of Black musical guests.[1] On the flip side, given the political efforts of the Black Arts Movement and Black Nationalism during the 1960s, did Wilson's provocative character do more harm than

45

good?[2] Did Geraldine's sashay appearance (she was liberated, flirtatious, and loud) help to reinstate racist stereotypes of African Americans often held by Caucasian Americans in this country for many years? According to *Ebony Magazine* publisher Lerone Bennett, Jr. that may have been the case. He states:

> There is a certain grim white humor [Irony], in the fact that the Black marches and demonstrations of the 1960s reached artistic fulfillment in the 1970s with Flip Wilson's Geraldine and Melvin Van Peebles's Sweetback, two provocative and insidious reincarnations of all the Sapphires and Studs of yesteryear (Bogle, 236).

Wilson's drag queen performance of Geraldine Jones (which included common stereotypes depicting the Black female as loud, bossy, and boisterous) confirmed a number of prejudicial assumptions regarding the Black female, and at the same time, debased the image of the Black gay male. "[Geraldine's] voice was the voice of Butterfly McQueen, who played the role of the slave in *Gone With the Wind*" (Garber, 298). In addition, Wilson's drag act raises questions pertaining to the performance of Black femininity and masculinity to all Americans. Is Black masculinity and authentic Blackness defined by physical stature? Class? Family structure? Political views? This chapter will examine these questions as well as the scholarship work of E. Patrick Johnson, and his argument concerning how several heterosexual Black male comedic actors have appropriated queerness to demean and delimit the parameters of authentic Black masculinity.

According to Johnson, "When black Americans have employed the rhetoric of black authenticity, the outcome has often been a political agenda that has excluded more voices than it has included" (3). The construct of a Black identity and the connection identity has to authenticity poses another problem for Johnson. He suggests that:

> if one were to look at blackness in the context of black American history, one would find that, even in relation to nationalism, the notion of an "authentic" blackness has always been contested: the discourse of "house niggers" vs. "field niggers"; Sourner Truth's insistence on black female subjectivity in relation to black polity; Booker T. Washington's call for vocational skill over W. E. B. Du Bois's "talented tenth"; Richard Wright's critique of Zora Neale Hurston's focus on the "folk" over the plight of the black man; Eldridge Cleaver's caustic attack on James Baldwin's homosexuality as "anti-black" and "anti-male"; urban northern's condescending attitudes toward rural southerns and vice versa; Malcolm X's militant call for black Americans to fight against white establishment "by any means necessary" over Martin Luther King Jr.'s reconciliatory "turn the other cheek"; and Jesse Jackson's "Rainbow Coalition" over Louis Farrakhan's "Nation of Islam." (4)

For Johnson, certain Black Americans within the Black community have taken it upon themselves to construct a definition of Black authenticity that does not reflect or validate the views of the community.[3] Furthermore, while Black America spends time contesting the construction of Blackness in order to further personal political agendas, Johnson asserts that White America continues to circulate derogatory tropes of Blackness that maintain Whiteness as the master trope of purity (4). Authenticity, then, is yet another trope manipulated for cultural and economic capital.

MINSTREL SHOWS IN NINETEENTH-CENTURY AMERICA

Early debates over the definition of Blackness stem back to the early minstrel shows from 1834 to the 1860s. According to Eric Lott, it was during this period that the "white [man's] fascination with commodified 'black bodies' developed" (27). Lott contends that the minstrel show evolved from a "white obsession with black (male) bodies" (23). Moreover, the White man's fascination of the Black body resulted in the appropriation of Black cultural materials that were ultimately used to promote slavery as amusing, right, and natural (23). Lott states that the first minstrel shows (which included the performance of White males in Black face in character roles as mammies) put narrative to a variety of uses, but they relied primarily on the objectification of Black characters in comic set pieces, repartee, and physical burlesque (28). Scholar Marjorie Garber agrees with Lott's assessment of Black face characters stating that, "most of the troupes were all-male, men who blacked [sic] their faces with burnt cork to sing, dance, and tell jokes in 'Negro' dialect" (276). Furthermore, Garber suggests that the minstrel shows of the nineteenth-century were the beginning of a new era of theatrical entertainment in America, commonly referred to today as transvestite theater (276).

   Lott places minstrelsy's early emphasis on what film theorists call "spectacle" rather than narrative. The spectacle consisted of the theatrical blocking of Black people at center stage for the fulfillment of white political desires and entertainment. Lott asserts:

> Black figures [male and female] became erotic objects both for other characters on stage and for spectators in the theater. . . . [M]instrel characters were simply trash-bin projections of white fantasy, vague fleshly signifiers that allowed whites to indulge at a distance all that they found repulsive and fearsome. (35–36)

For the duration of this period, the consciousness of "Blackness" was commodified into a marketable obsession of White curiosity, which confirms earlier arguments made by Johnson. Furthermore, Lott would agree with Johnson's assessment, regarding how the circulation of derogatory

tropes of Blackness maintains Whiteness as the master trope both economically and culturally.

EDDIE MURPHY: THE NEW COON?

The Reagan-led conservative administration in the White House during
the 1980s paved the way for the reemergence of "family values," while
simultaneously marginalizing those outside the heteronormative sphere
of family including gays, lesbians, single working women and single

**Figure 4.1.   Considered by many to be one of the best Black entertainers of all
time, Bert Williams is probably best known for his performances in blackface
from 1893–1921. Library of Congress, Prints & Photographs Division, Carl Van
Vechten Collection, reproduction number LC-DIG-ds-07363.**

parents (Johnson, 61). According to Johnson, the discourse surrounding homophobia during the 1980s was largely the result of conservative Reagan policies. Moreover, the insidious antigay pro-family sentiments promoted by the Reagan administration not only supported Whiteness as the master trope, but ironically also stimulated the career of a contentious Black comedian named Eddie Murphy.

Murphy's early comedic endeavors were not by any stretch of the imagination considered "family friendly." In fact, Murphy was notorious for making remarks routinely during his stand-up bits that would be considered inappropriate by the FCC. After achieving fame with *Saturday Night Live* and *Beverly Hills Cop*, Murphy released several film versions of his one man live performances such as *Delirious* (1983) and *Eddie Murphy: Raw* (1987). In *Raw*, his "I'm just out there" comments may be too far out there for some audiences:

> White people can't dance. I'm not being racist it's true. Just like when white people say black people have big lips, it's not racist it's true. Black people have big lips, white people can't dance. Some brothers will be in the club and white people are like, "What are those niggers doing in here?" They watchin' y'all dance. And they're like, "Look at these crazy muthafuckas." (1987)

Akin to the earlier argument posed by Lott, one could infer that Murphy's stand-up character during the 1980s became another minstrel cast member at center stage for the fulfillment of White political fantasies. Moreover, for Reagan-era audiences, his early screen characters may have even represented a flight from serious confrontations with racial tensions (Bogle, 281).

Johnson suggests that, "The popularity of comedian Eddie Murphy during the 1980s was no doubt fueled by the pervasive antigay, profamily sentiment of [the Reagan era]" (62). Murphy had a large white constituency from the very beginning, and by adding homophobic dialogue to his repertoire, his stand-up act ultimately became commodified, and sold as amusement. Thus, Murphy's White audiences were primed not only for the limp-wristed sissies but also for the general homophobia of his stand-up routines, including the irresponsible miseducation about how AIDS was contracted (62).

Johnson's concern with Murphy's showbiz humor stems from Murphy's 1983 HBO live performance, *Delirious*, recorded at Constitution Hall in Washington, DC, as well as comments Murphy made during his live performance of *Eddie Murphy: Raw*. Murphy's performance in *Delirious* is scripted with such homophobic comments as, "I'm afraid of gay people. Petrified. I have nightmares about gay people" (Johnson, 48). From a particular sketch in the 1987 film *Raw*, Murphy acknowledges the fact that the gay community is upset with him by stating, "I have pissed some gay people off and [they] are 'looking for [me]'"(Johnson, 62). What is problematic for Johnson is that within this same sketch, Murphy mimics a mob of effeminate gay men whose "radar" detects his arrival at the airport (63). Johnson avows that in this performance,

> Murphy-clad, ironically, in feminizing tight, lavender leather pants that prominently feature the ass he so desperately wants to hide from the faggots in his audience—camps up the performance by embodying this gay persona, pretending to be on top of the police car as the queeny "siren." The punchline for the joke, which incidentally, perpetuates the myth of the sex-crazed homosexual who wants nothing more than to fuck, comes when the gay cop commands Murphy to "spread'em," and commences to feel up his crotch and ass. (63)

It was based off these performances, according to Johnson, that Murphy gained a reputation as being homophobic. Although his aversion to homosexuality was evident, Eddie Murphy's in-depth knowledge of gay vernacular, produced rumors that questioned his sexuality.

Perhaps the repressed "Other" within Murphy is clearly seen in his drag performance in the film *Norbit* (2007). In the film, Murphy plays three characters: Norbit, Mr. Wong, and Rasputia. Norbit, who is portrayed as a normal person, was abandoned by his parents in 1967, and is adopted by Mr. Wong.[4] Mr. Wong owns an orphanage that eventually is sold to one of the former orphans, Kate Thomas, who was Norbit's childhood love. Norbit is in a precarious situation, given the fact that he is still in love with his childhood sweetheart, and he is married to Rasputia. Rasputia is a mammy type character whose plus-size appearance is so grotesque that it forces Norbit to pursue a relationship with the lighter hue, much slimmer Kate Thomas. Moreover, Rasputia's unattractive, overweight, desexed appearance and minstrel performance in the film supports the position by Eric Lott that "These 'female' bodies, it is true, were 'also' male, and minstrel performers did not hesitate to flirt with the homosexual content of blackface transvestism" (Lott, 27). Thus, the Black female body becomes part of the spectacle.

According to Johnson, Murphy's drag performance in films such as *Norbit* and *The Nutty Professor II: The Klumps* (Murphy's drag character is Ida Mae "Granny" Jensen, 1996) suggests a silent desire by Murphy to explore homosexuality, and questions Murphy's posture on Black heterosexuality and masculinity. Johnson suggests that, "In Murphy's performances, and perhaps in Murphy himself, the image of the black queer emerges in spite of the continual attempts of its murder at the hands of his heterosexual" (65). Contrary to what Murphy's parodies imply, perhaps the real spectacle for Johnson is the ongoing speculation concerning Murphy's association with transsexuals.

"TWO SNAPS UP": QUESTIONS OF MASCULINITY
AND STEREOTYPES IN THE TV PROGRAM *IN LIVING COLOR*

During the early 1990s, Rupert Murdock's FOX Television Network launched a comedy variety show called *In Living Color*.[5] The show, which was produced and directed by Keenan-Ivory Wayans, had a successful run on the network from 1990 to 1994. Several comedy sketches evolved from the series that ultimately launched the careers of comedians Jim Carrey, Tommy Davidson, Jamie Foxx, Kim Wayans, and "Fly Girl" dancer Jennifer Lopez. Two comedians in particular, Damon Wayans and David Allen Grier, had recurring roles in the popular skit "Men on Film." For Johnson, the commercial success of "Men on Film," which was based on stereotypes of gayness, sexual innuendos, and random misogynistic behavior, was an insult to the gay community.

In the skit, heterosexual comedians Damon Wayans and David Allen Grier portray two effeminate men, Blaine Edwards and Antoine Meriwether, who wear flashy chiffon blouses, tight pants, hair poufs, and feathered slippers (Johnson, 66). Johnson states that "because they never explicitly state they are gay, their pseudodrag garb along with their effeminate mannerisms [are] meant to signify their gayness" (66). Week after week, the two characters would review books, films, and other literary texts in a similar mode to reviews done by film critics Siskel and Ebert. However, rather than give a "two thumbs up" for a positive review, they appropriate a noncommunicative action that was once popular amongst Black gay men called "SNAP!" SNAP! is an expression used by Black gay males to signify an unanticipated and unexpected event. Similar to "Really," "Wow," or "Off the Hook" the meaning of the word varies depending on the context from which it is used. Furthermore, Johnson argues that the parody stereotypes all gays as "'queeny' and promiscuous in addition to perpetuating the myth that all gay men also hate women" (68). Johnson posits that within the context of the parody, misogyny becomes hyperbolic, propagating the illusion that women hating and homosexuality are somehow linked together.

Johnson's argument is problematic in that his assessment only briefly touches on the historical background regarding the "Snap," and he fails to call attention to the symbolic meaning behind the term within gay vernacular. In George C. Wolfe's play *The Colored Museum*, the exhibit entitled "The Gospel According [to] Miss Roj" features the drag queen character Miss Roj, who announces that he is a "Snap Queen" and that "Snapping comes from another galaxy as do all snap queens" (Elam, 294). Elam asserts that despite the complexity of Black homosexual experience, the drag queen Miss Roj is "Snapping" or "signifyin'" on the conventional, heterosexual world. "While the world of drag queen is commonly perceived as consisting of moral and spiritual degradation, sexual uncertainty and identity crisis, Miss Roj subverts these conceptions"(295).

Wolfe's character representation of Miss Roj cynically informs the audience of the power of the SNAP! in addition to chastising the spectators for their compliancy and failure to recognize their own cultural blindness (Elam, 295). In Johnson's defense, perhaps the real issue is not the question of symbolic meaning but rather the argument he makes on how authentic queerness can serve as a legitimate signifier of Blackness.

AUTHENTICITY AND SINCERITY
IN THE FILM *PARIS IS BURNING*

From drag nights to the drag Queen, the artistic expression of "voguing" at the Ball, *Paris Is Burning* (1990) is a powerful reflection of personal pride and celebration within the Black and Latino gay community. The film explores the highly structured Ball competition in which contestants are judged on specific themes, clothes, dancing ability, and keeping it (their drag performance) real. Within the construct of the "Ball," the film examines the roles of race, class, and gender in America. The expressive Ball culture that began in the transgender Black and Latino communities in New York has developed into a performative and social phenomenon that incorporates verbal skills and other creative elements such as dance, music, and fashion.

The film's success centers on the sincerity of interviews conducted by the filmmaker (Jennie Livingston) with the Ball communal members. Many of the performers in *Paris Is Burning* articulate their commitment to speaking out about their desired social identities with personal pride. The director does an excellent job taking the viewer for a "walk around the Ball" which consists of a series of interviews with Ball participants (the "Walk" is similar to a walk or strut on a fashion runway). Contrary to the stereotypical gay caricature image of the drag queen that has been appropriated and abused by the mainstream media and culture, these drag participants (also known as ball community members) express their concerns about poverty as well as their enthusiasm for Ball culture through personal monologues.

The concept of Ball culture parlays into another complex exploration that focuses on the meaning of family and home. "Banned from both the public spaces of heterosexual black 'home' and the white gay clubs, black gay men and women create private places (the night club, another gay person's house, a ball house, etc.) to create community" (82). Johnson argues that the concept of "house" in Black gay vernacular denotes a safe haven for Black men who may be homeless or are in need of shelter. Moreover, Johnson states that "the black gay house-dwellers create communitas by maintaining the heteronormative structure concept of house while at the same time subverting the hegemonic limitations on 'house' by appropriating the heteronormative familial and domestic connotations of the term in relation to 'home'" (84). Johnson's definition of communitas reflects a philosophical position of joint ownership by which people share in common social, economic, and political interests.

In the film *The Wizard of Oz*, Dorothy dreams of the day when she can return to her home town of Kansas. In her dream, she repeats the phrase "There's no place like home." Johnson suggests a similar dream exists within the Black gay community. He asserts that for the dream to become a reality, a productive rebuilding of home must take place through a Black gay vernacular performance. Johnson states, "Through discourse that draws from on the most innovative vernacular practices of black culture and the campy idioms and codes of black gay culture, black men have created 'houses' that allow them to go home 'as who they are . . .'" (102). For Johnson, the rebirth of home creates a performative stage that allows for the appropriation of the heteronormative term "mother." The house is also a surrogate family for Black and Latino gay youth, and it provides a space for acceptance of Black gay men who have been alienated from their biological families because of their sexuality. In the *Wizard of Oz*, Dorothy's return to Kansas occurs once she clicks her heels together and repeats the phrase, "There's no place like home." For Johnson, however, the return to home may imply private spaces that permit Black gay men to feel comfortable expressing their sexuality or adopting dress codes that signify their membership as members of particular sexual communities (82).

THE NEW "DRAG" MAMMIES: DRAG PERFORMANCES BY MARTIN LAWRENCE AND TYLER PERRY

In the blockbuster film *Big Momma's House*, Martin Lawrence plays an undercover cop who poses as a heavyset woman known to family and friends as Big Momma. The storyline of the film *drags* the spectator through the "under padding, makeup, and wig" which are the key essentials in the depiction of Lawrence's drag character. The camera treats the real Big Momma in the film (played by Ella Mitchell), mercilessly, especially in a bathroom sequence where she is partially nude. The framing of shots displays an image of a grotesquely overweight woman with layers of fat around her waist and hips. Lawrence, as the pretend Big Momma, is seen as a Mammy figure that is quick to nurture and protect, displaying no type of enthralling sexuality (Bogle, 398).

Tyler Perry, the latest phenomenon, has written, directed, and produced several films that include Black men wearing plus-size pantyhose parading around as their grandmothers. His claim to the fame is the character Medea. In *Diary of a Mad Black Woman*, Charles McCarter (Steve Harris) and his wife Helen (Kimberly Elise) are attending an awards banquet where Charles is receiving an award for the most outstanding lawyer in Atlanta. They are about to celebrate their eighteenth wedding anniversary when Helen comes home to find her clothes packed up in a U-Haul van parked in the driveway. Unbeknownst to Helen, there is now a new wardrobe of designer clothes in the closet representing a new relationship for her husband. Bottom-line, Charles is divorcing Helen for a younger woman. Helen moves in with her grandmother Medea (Tyler Perry), an older woman who does not put up with any nonsense from anyone. Additionally, if things get too out hand, she will make use of the gun that she has in her possession.

In *Medea Goes to Jail* (2009), Medea, despite her circumstances (she gets sent to the jail), gives her trademark advice and wisdom to her friends and family as they learn the importance of letting go, moving on, and forgiveness. In the film *Meet the Browns* (2008), Perry again plays the character role Medea. The storyline focuses on a single mother (a character named Brenda) living in the inner city of Chicago. Brenda has struggled for years to make ends meet and keep her three kids off the street. When she is laid off with no warning, she starts losing hope for the first time until a letter arrives announcing the death of a father she has never met. Desperate for any kind of help, Brenda takes her family to Georgia for the funeral. However, nothing could have prepared her for the Browns, her father's high-spirited, obtuse, Southern family. The story (like many of Perry's films) is adapted from his stage play *Meet the Browns*.[6] "Urban audiences have lined up in droves to enjoy his traditional formula of romantic, family-centered melodrama—spiced with over-the-top, insult-hurling characters—which he honed years ago writing plays that were targeted to black churchgoers" (Braxton, *L.A. Times*).

In *Meet the Browns*, Perry (as he does in other films) not only plays the drag role Medea, but he plays a second character role in the film as Uncle Joe. A familiar trope, the cross between male and female roles played by Lawrence, Murphy, and Perry create a performance of masculinity that embodies a hyper-masculine female character. In several films, the male character is portrayed as being weak and emasculate versus the domineering portrayal of the drag queen.

According to *L.A. Times* writer Greg Braxton, there are some Black people within the film industry who are not impressed with Tyler Perry's creative talents:

> Despite the popularity of Perry's films, and the message of faith, family togetherness, and perseverance against seemingly overwhelming odds, the celebration and support within the black film community for his so called "positive messages" has been low-key. Perry's popularity—and the images he has presented, (particularly his Medea character), has become a contentious issue for independent Black filmmakers.

The boisterous, Mammy type grandmother laden with heavy makeup has been embraced by the Hollywood mainstream community, ultimately closing the door for the aspiring Black filmmaker who would like to produce dramatic, personal stories with complexity, versus the boorish themes so often displayed in the Perry movies.

CONCLUDING THOUGHTS

According to Maurice Wallace, given the deeply psychic politics of race characterizing our (post) modern experience, there can be little question that our present conceptions of masculinity in the West owe as much to certain racial preoccupations as they do the sexual ones that vex the very iteration "homological" itself (2).

Wallace would agree with Lott's analysis that White America's obsession with Blackness has produced a mode of bigotry that eventually resulted in the Black body becoming a part of the drag performance. The spectacle for Black men in Hollywood films includes the overt drag roles they play. These ultimately reflect an ambivalence about gays and lesbians in Black culture and an ambivalence about Black males in White culture (Garber, 300). In the case of the film *Paris Is Burning*, Judith Butler puts forward a similar argument on how the spectacle (in this case, pretentious drag performances) can create contradictions of realness. She states, "At best, it seems, drag is a site of a certain ambivalence, one which reflects the more general situation of being implicated in the regimes of power by which one is constituted and, hence, of being implicated to the very regimes of power that one opposes" (125). Dissimilar to the drag performances done by Black men in Hollywood films, for the viewers of *Paris Is Burning*, the drag show may appear to be artificial. Nevertheless, it achieves realness for the ball participants.

In the same way Griffith's spectacle *Birth of a Nation* (1915) created mythic types of Blackness such as coons, toms, and Mammies, Johnson argues parodies such as *Men on Film* "discredits gayness as a legitimate signifier of Blackness" (72). Moreover, I contend that the new images of the Black comedic drag queen in television and film, represents a form of minstrel castration that is comparable to the characters produced on stage during the early minstrel shows.[7] Film critic David Brochette notes:

> Hollywood has consistently treated the Black gay character as a [mammy]/buddy, an almost always finger-snapping queen whose entire presence is defined by hilarity. "Auntie Tom" roles conflate misogyny and homophobia in what is, in some circles, a sure-fire comic formula. (Garber, 300)

These negative depictions are not only demeaning to Black gay culture, but also to the identity and ideality of the Black female.

From the *Last Night on Earth*, Bill T. Jones states:

> You think I'm going to please you, but 'm going to show you some-
> thing we both have trouble looking at. It's in my legs and hips, my face
> filled with clouds passing to reveal the sun, and now clouds again, it's
> in my voice. Perhaps I am pretending, but this is my habitat, this place
> of illusion. (Wallace, 161)

Conceivably, for Johnson, the place of illusion is the process by which
Black masculinity secures its power by repudiating the homosexual Other, and ironically conjoining masculine gender identification with homosexual identification. Johnson has established a starting point for discourse regarding a new definition of authentic Blackness and authentic
masculinity. Moreover, his argument that Blackness and Black masculinity need not follow normative standards is firm. Even though Johnson
diffuses the myth that the only true Black man is the normatively masculine male, there are still questions posed within the title of this chapter
regarding who was responsible for burning down the authenticity and
sincerity of Paris, and why do Black comedians like to perform in drag?
Perhaps, if you were to ask Big Momma, Medea, Rasputia, or even Geraldine, all four would say, "The *devil* made us do it."[8]

> The devil led him up to a high place and showed him in an instant all
> the kingdoms of the world. And he said to him, "I will give you all
> their authority and splendor; it has been given to me, and I can give it
> to anyone I want to. If you worship me, it will all be yours. . . . When
> the devil had finished all this tempting, he left him until an opportune
> time."
>
> —Luke 4:5–7; 13 (*NIV*)

NOTES

1. The program included Black entertainers such as Isaac Hayes, The Temptations,
and James Brown.

2. BAM insisted that Black Art gave the Black community some political and social
direction. Participants in the Black Arts Movement often belittled those involved in the
Harlem Renaissance for what they considered to be a disconnection with African
American people. In 1971, BAM participant Haki Madhubuti in his essay, "Renaissance I To Renaissance III? An Introduction" states "[T]he black arts movement in the
twenties was of a minimal influence . . . more whites knew about what was happening
than brothers and sisters" (Collins and Crawford, 13).

3. Who speaks for me? Varied opinions cause division within the Black community. Examples include the controversy regarding who should vote for Barack Obama
in 2008. Some Blacks were for Obama, some were for Hillary, and God forbid if any
were for McCain.

4. This raises another question regarding Murphy's definition of normativity.

5. I find it interesting that Rupert Murdock, who is considered to be one of the
most conservative men in the media, had one of the most controversial networks
during the 1990s. The FOX Network gave birth to shows such as *In Living Color*, *The
Tracey Ullman Show*, *Married with Children*, and *The Simpsons*.

6. The film *Meet the Browns* grossed more than $20 million during the opening
weekend at the box office.

7. I refer to these new images as "Castrated Buffoons."

8. The devil in this case refers to capitalism and establishes the point raised by Garber that female impersonators were the best paid performers in the minstrel company (276).

FIVE

The Scarface Identity

*Rap Gone Wild, Cash Money Bruthas,
and Niggas killin' Nigga(z) on da Streets*

Rob Prince Obey and David L. Moody

Gonna lay down my sword and shield, Down by the riverside, Down
by the Riverside, I ain't gonna study war no more.
— "Gonna Lay Down My Burdens," by the Fisk Jubilee Singers

Violent images on the silver screen have been debated in cinematic studies for some time. Critics frequently question whether violent content can
lead to contentious behavior in an individual. Alternatively, considering
the existing discourse surrounding the construction of Black masculine
identity in America, Brian DePalma's 1983 gangster epic *Scarface* tops the
list of narratives that should be included for discussion. Why does the
film *Scarface* resonant so strongly with young Black males who consider
themselves members of the hip hop generation? What is the film's cultural connection to this particular audience? A substantive investigation is
required on the appropriate historical, psychological, and socio-economic
factors that permit mostly underprivileged young Black men to favorably
receive this unique text and adopt *Scarface*'s Tony Montana as the ultimate "Gangsta Super Hero" of the ghetto.

Accordingly, it was *Scarface*'s effect, the film's remarkable intervention
in the existing social fabric of America, that is its greatest legacy. For at
the soul of the film are its relentless thematic images of violence, drug
use, and capitalism in America. Specifically, the film focuses on the use of
violence as a strategic weapon of choice to change lives for the better, as

exampled by the rags-to-riches life of the film's hero and gangsta identity role model Tony Montana (played by Al Pacino).

Violence championed in *Scarface* serves several functions for the hip hop community. Firstly, violence represents a hegemonic environment that preys on the weak (one can dominate as well as survive against the odds) and promotes the tenants of capitalism as the ultimate ideology. Thus, this particular theme was underscored by the film's marketing tag line "He loved the American Dream . . . with a vengeance." Secondly, the violent behavior serves to legitimize the survival of the fittest mentality and a sense of ownership (or entitlement) upheld by Black youth within the inner cities of America. Finally, the *Scarface* narrative inspired the re-emergence of a new epoch of Black masculine identity similar to the aggressive style of behavior that was common in the 1970s *Blaxploitation* cinema. Characters such as John Shaft (*Shaft*, 1971), Youngblood Priest in *Super Fly* (1972) and Tommy Gibbs in *Black Caesar* (1974) depicted a tough guy, mobster type mentality which is often associated with the hip hop community. Moreover, from a Black female perspective, one could argue that the sassy personalities of hip hop artists Missy Elliott and Mary J. Blige share similar behavioral/character traits to fictional heroines such as Teresa Graves' Christie Love from the made-for-TV films *Get Christie Love!* (1974–1975), Tamera Dobson's *Cleopatra Jones*, and the badass fe-male detective vigilante characters played by Pam Greer (*Coffy*, 1973; *Foxy Brown*, 1974; *Sheba, Baby*, 1975).

Historically, the depicted images of rogue detectives, hustlers, and pimps in the *Blaxploitation* films gave birth to the early beginnings of the hip hop gangsta-criminal persona, an identity which has dominated Black themed films dating back to *New Jack City* in 1991. Hollywood glorification of the hip hop "gangsta" (inner city slang for gangster) res-urrected the worst Black male stereotypes America has created. Conse-quently, with murder-per-day horrors in places such as Detroit, south central Los Angeles, and Chicago (Chicago is perhaps America's best example of ongoing domestic terrorism), there appears to be no end in sight to gang related killings. Ironically, even with the election of a Black American to the office of President of the United States, the worst com-munal offenses of gang related crime happens to occur on President Oba-ma's own home turf—the streets of Chicago.

As a result of the ghetto-centric narratives commonly seen in the *Blax-ploitation* films, Hollywood producers were successful at constructing several Black male superheroes whose ultimate goals were to achieve pre-ordained victories over "The White Man," while at the same time participating in verboten sexual acts with White women. Thematically speaking, *Blaxploitation* films gave Black American males (who were at the forefront of the rioting during the 1960s) an opportunity to fantasize about a perfect world in which they were the powerful masters of all they surveyed. The characters in these films were in control of their own destinies which included:

- The control of "Whitey"
- The ability to promote and engage in misogynistic activities
- The ultimate prize—the forbidden fruit (sexual activity with the White female)

However, unlike the real life victories of the Civil Rights Movement, these cinematic coups only lasted about two hours; afterwards audience members had to leave the obscurity of the theater to go out and face the harsh realities of street life. From the documentary film *The Black Power Mixtape: 1965–1975* (2010), Talib Kweli states, "People who are poor and oppressed, they focus on survival. The drugs seem like an easy escape route." Gang association has become a new way for youth to meet the challenges associated with poverty and life on the streets; moreover, gangs provide profitable pecuniary opportunities, eminence, and respect—especially for youths who lack the essential educational and job skills necessary for employment.

HIP HOP MALE AUDIENCE PSYCHOLOGY

When the body of scholarship that might lend credence to a definitive critical understanding of hip hop audience psychology was considered, it was found that existing urban gangsta behaviors such as a propensity for violence and consistently acting emotionless and detached (cool posing) are the result of long term, systemic social and economic oppression that can be traced back to institutionalized slavery. The Black male experience in America is one in which the kidnap victim (slavery was considered to be a form of forced immigration, thus the reference to kidnapping) now freed, becomes both feared and reviled because of his anger and search for social justice throughout society. Consequently, Hollywood's response to the Black male experience in America in the 1970s resulted in the construct of Black male super heroes portrayed as pimps, drug dealers, gangsters, and hyper-masculine male characters. Unfortunately, these new images were similar to the brutal Black buck characters depicted in the early racist era of cinema; in particular, in D. W. Griffith's film *Birth of Nation* (1915). The Black bucks, according to film historian Donald Bogle, "were always big, baadddd niggers, oversexed and savage, violent and frenzied as they lust for white flesh" (14). Subsequently, the sins of the Black buck (which typically center on the lust for White female flesh) created a hostile environment; setting the stage for the classic battle between White America (good) and Black America (evil). Furthermore, Bogle also states that Black themed films during the 1970s were, for the most part:

> [H]eady male action fantasies, with tenacious buck protagonist per-
> forming deeds of derring-do, while self-righteously giving lip service
> to the idea of political commitment. The films would have us to believe
> the heroes were out to clean up the ghetto of all its ills. Actually, the
> best way to have cleaned up the ghetto might have been to have first
> rounded up the producers of some of these vehicles. (241)

Thus, Hollywood planted a mendacious seed with audience members
that depicted the Black male as a feared predator pursuing potential pay-
back against his tormentor.

Therefore, these circumstances comprise the foundation for an understanding of why Black males of hip hop have connected with *Scarface* at
the expense of former Black heroes. This particular audience's reaction to
the film is based on its world view; one that is drenched in hopelessness,
despair, and violence. However, one could argue that a film which por-
trays a hero who overcomes his despotic situation, conquers, and becomes filthy rich symbolizes a fairy tale ending that would appeal to
most deprived Black males on the streets who are not only looking for a
pair of glass slippers but also a pair of new Nikes as well.

American Black masculinity is a tree rooted by the legacy of African
enslavement. As stated earlier, African males were kidnapped and for-
cibly brought to the Americas as slaves—their cultural identities were
taken away and replaced with a European conception of manhood that
characterized Black males as inferior beings—closer to King Kong than
mankind.[1] Therefore, as the process that created contemporary Black
male identity is deconstructed and shredded from the cloth of White
patriarchy, the gangsta faction of this identity is a violent pathology
predicated on a potent brew of self-hatred. Additionally, since the transition from African masculine values to European masculine values occurred in chains at gunpoint, the majority of academic literature within
the discourse chronicles a justification of the inevitable psychological outcome for men forced to live in an environment so hostile to their well-
being; the only logical expectations were self-hate and violent actions of
vengeance and retribution.

According to Camara Harrell, a professor of psychology at Howard
University, Black Americans perform a mental response to racism. Harrell calls this response "Manichean" psychology, a term he created from
the significant work of renowned Black psychiatrist Franz Fanon. Harrell
explains the concept, suggesting that:

> The total expression of modern racism creates a Manichean universe in
> which the oppressed are doomed to live out their lives. In his discus-
> sion of racism and psychopathology, Fanon used the term Manichean
> to describe the world of the colonized. In fact, the adherents of the
> teachings of Manicheaus in the third century A.D. saw an inherent
> conflict between light and darkness. The Manicheans conceived of
> blackness and things associated with it as evil. Whiteness, or light,

became associated with good. It is not difficult to see how the Manichean order manifests itself along racial lines. People of African descent become associated with evil and inferiority.[2]

For Black males, this hybrid of western masculinity was doomed to never attain the White archetype. The lack of melanin (which caused pale, White skin) indicated flawlessness, while dark skin was reviled. Long hair, blue eyes, and thin lips and noses were idealized. White Americans were at odds with prototypical features, so bodies for the Black Americans were purposefully illustrated as having ape like features. These cruel stereotypes were nurtured by centuries of systematic abuse within different systems of control maintained by the ruling classes; first under the total control of the slave system and then after emancipation. Consequently, the former slaves now faced a new system of oppression in the form of "Jim Crow" segregation within the former Confederate states. This legal discrimination lasted nearly a century until it was dismantled by the work of Civil Rights advocates. Hence, when the final barriers began to crumble, Blacks were treated as though they were an infectious disease let loose upon the unsuspecting populace in America. In particular, Black men were feared by White men due to the longstanding myths Whites themselves had created about Black masculinity, especially those involving their desire for White women, sexual prowess, and genital size.

THE COOL POSE VERSUS BLACK MALE RAGE

In real life, the cool pose is a psychological theory which catalogs certain types of observable behavior patterns performed by Black males, most of whom live in the inner city. Moreover, the perception of being cool is probably the most consistent form of male behaviors in film history. Likewise, the cool pose proves to be an extremely useful tool in identifying those key moments in *Scarface* that resonated at the highest level of influence for the hip hop spectator in terms of audience reception. Acting cool is a skill that must be perfected by gangsta males who wish to be successful on the street. According to noted sociologist William Julius Wilson, "The evolution of cool-pose culture, with its emphasis on appearance and fashion, sexual conquests, and partying" might explain the role cultural traits play on the social and economic outcomes of young Black males (149–50).

In the discourse on Black masculinity, cool posing is a foundational element—as stated previously, acting cool in cinematic terms symbolizes valor. Arguably, without the element of cool posing, the entirety of the *Scarface* narrative would have most likely been ignored over time by the Black male audience. Instead, Montana's cool under fire approach to problems were in the best traditions of the Hollywood hyper-masculine persona, and his actions demonstrated those values the gangsta holds close.

Gender scholar Sharon R. Bird expresses the opinion that because of hegemonic masculinity and its inherently competitive base, men are often incapable of expressing emotions for fear of being thought of as weak, a key outcome of the cool pose.[3] One of the observations that can be made about *Scarface*'s Tony Montana is that he is very open about expressing his feelings, yet he is not perceived by audience members as weak. On the one hand, Montana demonstrates a sincere love for Elvira Hancock and his sister Gina; however, he balances any tenderness (and potential signs of weakness) he might exhibit with powerful displays of stark rage—evident by the murder of his best friend Manolo. As a result, it's Tony Montana's hostility (illustrated in the film by his heinous acts of murder) that male hip hop audience members found both stimulating and psychologically fulfilling because it connected to their daily lives.

According to actor Mekhai Phifer in an interview from the documentary *Def Jam Presents Scarface: Origins of a Hip Hop Classic* (2003): "*Scarface* represented the capitalistic society that we live in. . . . But you know, it also represented that we don't have to conform to society in order to quote, unquote, make it." From the same documentary rapper Nas also states, "We are all savages in pursuit of the American Dream. . . . Rappers relate to that because that's how we come up." Successful rappers (especially street rappers) maintain that Tony Montana's rags to riches story is similar to theirs. They identify with and are motivated by "another Cat making it [regardless] of how he was getting it" (Sean P. Diddy Combs).

A great number of scholars have critiqued Black male rage—of notable interest is the work of philosopher Tommy L. Lott. In his collection of essays on the constructions of race and class, particularly from his work *The Invention of Race*, Lott writes:

> Black urban males have been depicted in mass media as the number-one criminal threat to America. The social and political function of mass media's image of the so-called "underclass" is to routinely validate this claim. The mass media's labeling of black men as criminals serves in the consciousness of many whites as a justification of anti-black vigilantism.[4] (123)

Lott goes on to identify what he sees as the primary underlying factor contextualizing all Black cultural resistance movements—poverty, and the powerlessness that accompanies this condition. Lott explains, "As long as black urban youth in extreme poverty neighborhoods see themselves trapped under America's apartheid their cultural expressions will continue to exhibit elements of resistance."[5]

The conditions of extreme poverty faced by Black youth in our urban ghettos appear to have created warriors who oppose the status quo and would rather die than give in to an oppressive White male dominated hegemonic society. Cornel West's essay "Nihilism in Black America" echoes this sentiment further. West states:

> We must acknowledge that structures and behavior are inseparable, that institutions and values go hand in hand. *How people act and live is shaped*—though in no way dictated or determined—*by the larger circumstances in which they find themselves.*[6] (37)

The hip hop male's "larger circumstances," the poverty and despair of his daily existence, certainly created the "elements of resistance" that Lott referred to.

From the 1960s uprisings in Watts to the Hough riots in Cleveland, music and lyrics have always appeared to lead the way in the expression of anguish and anger for Black Americans. Moreover, early Gangsta rappers such as the godfather of the genre, Philly product Schooly D, have been lyrically presenting many visual symbols that represent the resistance of young Black males attempting to survive the rough and tumble life within their impoverished residential areas. However, after the elimination of the 1970s heroic images that Black audiences could root for, *Scarface* should be considered an important benchmark in the timeline of socioeconomic justice in America. The film met an unfulfilled need for a specific target demographic of Black males looking for something to cheer for. This was, at best, a problematic moment of self-identification and reassurance.

Ironically, *Scarface* was a film without a single meaningful image (positive or negative) of Blackness. Yet the film has become a powerful influence and cult classic within a segment of the Black population that might be easily influenced because of its tender age (Black males eighteen to twenty-four). Moreover, the psychological connection between *Scarface* and its audience might also be considered a predictably logical progression toward more violent behavior, or at the very least, confirmation of an ongoing construct of masculine identity that is determined to protect its own "homies" regardless of the final outcome. Alternatively, this gravitation towards self-preservation resulted in the formation of Black gangs such as the Black P. Stone Nation (aka Blackstone Rangers) of Chicago, thus creating a new vision and structure of Black organized crime with a code of the streets not seen since Bumpy Johnson controlled Harlem.

THE CODE OF THE STREETS

Elijah Anderson is one of the many scholars who study the socio-psychological aspects of Black male identity formation. His *Code of the Streets*[7] is a brilliant ethnographic tour de force. The "code of the street" provided all residents of the ghetto, be they gang bangers, wannabes, or non-affiliated "civilians" alike, an extremely useful set of survival rules. Ethnologist Terry Williams also connected these rules to the harsh economic conditions ghetto residents are forced to live under. He offers that the residents thought of themselves as hostages in an ongoing war of attrition. Consequently, he writes that observers should

> keep in mind the effect of economic isolation on an inner city community. The increasingly popular view among minorities (and increasingly the majority) is that they, as poor people, are viewed by the larger society as superfluous and expendable and that they are being killed off in a sort of triage operation, victims of a kind of low-intensity war.[8] (13)

Under these living conditions, young Black males strategized to become predators, and not prey, within their subculture. As American University political scientist Clarence Lusane observed, "Street culture, with its masculinist dimensions on full throttle, criss-crosses the black community at a number of class and social levels"[9] (89). Lusane goes on to point out that this "outlaw culture" has won the battle, between traditional moral values and a code that is in opposition to the rule of law, in the ghetto territories. The term "outlaw culture" has come to define gangsta ideology. bell hooks, in fact, used the term as a book title—other scholars, including Black Studies professor Mark Naison, have signified its cultural meaning through their own interpretive applications.[10] For example, while making an observation about Black inner city lawlessness Naison cautions that:

> An outlaw culture has emerged among low-income black youth that has rejected African-American communal norms in favor of the predatory individualism of the capitalist marketplace. These youngsters living in neighborhoods bereft of resources and hope, have embraced a doctrine of "might makes right" that converts everyone into a potential victim.[11] (128)

Scholars in the discourse have been found presenting terms and definitions such as "outlaw culture" "low-intensity war," "victims," "lumpen street culture," "submerged tenth," and "racial contract" to describe ghetto residents as well as their desperate conditions and experiences.

Here exegetical usages of "war zone," "ghetto territories," "oppression," "police occupation," and "White patriarchal tactics" have suggested considering the ghetto as a geographical area in which ongoing martial combat occurs proves to be as descriptive. By their own word choices, scholars appear to agree that both outlaws and victims exist in the ghetto. Furthermore, residents are economically and socially adrift due to past and current failures of private and public sector policy makers.[12]

Thus, a cultural fuse that has been waiting to be lit since the riots of the 1960s has ignited in the form of gangsta hip hop. Moreover, for the hip hop audience, *Scarface* became the latest historical benchmark in the ongoing chronicles of young Black male rage. Interpreting Justice Roger B. Taney's majority opinion in the Dred Scott Supreme Court decision of 1857, hip hop males of the gangsta lifestyle decided that since society was not going to respect them, there was no law that *they* were bound to respect, except their own.

THE GANGSTA: ALL I HAVE IN THIS WORLD IS . . .

DJ Ready Red, a leader in the rap group *The Geto Boys*, caused the gangsta identity to take a giant leap towards universality.[13] Decoding the film as a symbol for the angry warrior within, Red's deft rap sampling made the phrase "Balls and My Word" uttered by Tony Montana during a key moment in *Scarface* a common signifier. From *The Geto Boys*'s 1988 album *Making Trouble*, "Balls and My Word" lyrically offered repetitive beats that reflected the essence of Tony Montana's character. Montana worked the system, however, he felt the system of capitalism served one purpose, declaring: "You know what capitalism is? Getting fucked!" (IMDb). Therefore, telling the truth (even within the context of a lie) was a critical component to the construct of his gettocentric character. Either you fuck the system (according to Tony Montana) or the system will fuck you. Authenticity for rappers is predicated on being real and not getting played—thus, "Balls and My Word" resonated with Black males who understood the connection between themselves and the film. Additionally, the phrase also made reference to the lack of material possessions acquired by Black males who considered themselves trapped within the dark poverty of ghetto life.

However, despite the knowledge that the term resonated, no one had ever used it before as a cultural reference. This newness made its use cool to say, a signature for all similarly situated young men to acknowledge, through adherence, that a separate system of values existed, a warrior code constructed of sheer will. This code had proven to be historically indispensable to those seeking a fighting chance for survival in the ghettos of urban America.[14] Continual viewings of *Scarface* by hip hop males created more and more useful interpretations of the film's semiotic representations, specifically those scenes in which Tony Montana's loyalty to this system of values—a real life "code of honor" that mainstream audiences had become familiar with through Hollywood's gangster films—was depicted. The code was evident in films such as Martin Scorsese's *Goodfellas*, *The Godfather* films of Francis Ford Coppola, and in two HBO cable television series: *The Sopranos* and the gritty Baltimore based narco-drama *The Wire*. Consequently, because of the popularity of these films and programs with Black audiences, young Black males, in particular, developed an awareness and affinity for the code of honor.

These narratives constructed a reservoir of information, some fictional and some factual, causing audiences to believe all gangsters were, at once, an army *and* a family—an interwoven collective of men that adhered to a code that appeared to incorporate both honor and justice as established business practices in criminal capitalism. But it is their belief in this system, because these young men see themselves as warriors in an unending conflict, that forms the foundation of hip hop male gangsta identity.[15] *Scarface's* Tony Montana would become the symbol of that identity. What hip hop males concluded was that Tony's motivation paralleled their own. As represented in the film, Montana's mantra of success by any means necessary excited the young male audience. This pleasure is received in part because their life experience of poverty naturally would result in fantasies that focused on gaining wealth and power. As suggested by Stuart Hall's work on decoding, these desires were brought into viewing by the audience as a part of their psychological makeup.[16]

These fantasies created a crucial space for negotiation and bonding with the film as the audience's desire to be free from poverty and powerlessness formed a relationship with those parts of the hero's journey which best visualized consummations of that desire. According to apparatus theory, it was within this space that the formation of a long term emotional bond occurred between spectator and film.[17] In film studies, apparatus theory seeks to explain the relationship between the text, its audience, and the influence of ancillary material circumstances, such as what events are occurring at the time the film is viewed and the emotions individual audience members bring to the viewing.[18] Moreover, apparatus theory also informs the discourse on Black masculinity in that it explains the great extent to which the Black male audience is influenced during a film viewing by the depth of emotional circumstances that each audience brings into the viewing. While this is true for any film and every viewing, the experience is heightened when an audience senses that what it is seeing has already been experienced outside the viewing.

In the case of *Scarface*, Tony Montana was the first opportunity for hip hop males to view their fantasy—the idealized symbolic representations of what they wanted to become was their generation's *Shaft*. Despite being a work of fiction, *Scarface's* position within the cinematic apparatus allowed the male audience to see a spectacular version on the screen of both their current economic conditions and their aspirations. As is the case in any Cinderella archetype, *Scarface* gave hip hop males the confidence to believe their fantasies could come true, if they could just sell enough drugs and live a reasonable amount of time to spend some of the money they earned. The life or death struggles of young men in mortal combat on the streets allowed *Scarface* to become a Nietzschian philosophical metaphor for the ghetto bred male's search for the perfected masculine street identity, one that would be cool enough, and tough enough, for him to survive. *Scarface's* function as a role model would occur in large part to the luck of timing; the film and gangsta rap first appeared at practically the same time and thus they could mature together. This co-existing maturation is important to understanding the development of an identity construction that would create the gangsta.

THE *SCARFACE* IDENTITY:
"SAY HELLO TO MY LITTLE FRIEND"

The root causes of gangsta behavior were suggested earlier and all of the factors mentioned appear obvious as they had been persistent. Furthermore, the socio-economic conditions inherent in ghetto life were horrific. The residents who lived there were trapped in a prison without walls— moreover, their desire to move from a morose situation was restricted because of a lack of resources. In order to subsist, residents are often subjected to contempt and bullying tactics by local law enforcement officials. This unforgivingly dangerous landscape causes its residents to employ various methods to ensure their survival. Thus, the long term acute state of poverty within the ghetto territories fosters self-hatred and other psychopathies amongst the victims. There have been a number of terms utilized to describe the ghetto's cultural, social, and economic condition including "panopticon," "war zone," and "urban jungle." All of these descriptions are useful in contextualizing the hip hop segment of the *Scarface* audience but really do not serve to capture the essence of this phenomenon of resonance.

The hip hop male gangsta is forced to construct a working relationship with a hostile living environment controlled by an unsympathetic society. Gangsta behavior, specifically violence, thus should be considered as a predictable outcome in that it adheres to a set of values which are a collective reaction to this malady. Because films are powerful agents for mimicry, *Scarface* simply glorified already existing feelings that were brought into the theater by the audience. This glorification of violence and anti-social behavior greatly amplified those internal feelings through the machinations of the apparatus theory and then, like a great coach's halftime speech, sent the segment of the *Scarface* audience that was so inclined back out into "The Game" more determined than ever to get rich or die trying.

In an attempt to articulate the specific values that are common between *Scarface* and its hip hop male audience, the term "*Scarface* Identity" should prove useful. The "Identity" reflects a cause and effect approach to understanding the resonation between film and audience. Using the term provides a means to understand why the philosophical underpinnings of the film, a reflection of American hegemony gained through violence, are in such great use today. For example, having reviewed potential historical and contemporary causes for Black male rage, we can easily apply the gangsta principles adhered to in the film (i.e., drug based jobs in lieu of unemployment and violence based lives due to environment) as contributing factors to the creation of the *Scarface* Identity.

The gangsta does not want to be in his circumstance—how could he? In fact, everyone who can escape the ghetto panopticon runs for their lives. The *Scarface* Identity thus serves as an explanatory phrase, one that can be used as a tool to underscore how and why certain values are currently maintained (and have been historically maintained) by Black men who reside in the inner city. The "Identity" is an amalgamation of basic gangsta values—being cool, being tough, and acquiring respect.[19] However, it has become so much more than values. Several non-academic interrogations of Black manhood were also found to be extremely useful to coining this term, especially two documentary films: *Tough Guise: Violence, Media, and the Crisis in Masculinity* (1999), written and produced by Jackson Katz, and Byron Hurt's *Hip Hop: Beyond Beats and Rhymes* (2006). Hurt's film is unique in that it was produced by a young Black male from the hip hop generation who took great care to allow other hip hop aged Black males a voice to tell their own stories. *Hip Hop: Beyond Beats and Rhymes* also included interviews with scholars who have given focus to hip hop, including the prolific Michael Eric Dyson, who was quick to point out in the film that the gangsta lifestyle was part of a long tradition of violent behavior in America.

The *Scarface* Identity is an outcome of history and given the film's subject matter, *Scarface* would appear a text unworthy of any critical acclaim; however, the film's target audience has placed it at the top of the list of films that have captured the spirit of the hip hop culture. The *Scarface* Identity recognizes gangsta behavior that is rooted in slavery, capitalism, socio-political determinations, and everyday heteronormative cultural expectations. As evidenced by the agreement amongst the most prominent of the film studies reception theorists, the result of this narrative is that the representations of the gangsta's code of honor within *Scarface* provides an infomercial type instruction for (and reinforcement of) values necessary for the ongoing survival of the hip hop male audience once they leave the viewing experience.[20] This audience, due to serious shortcomings in their collective long term emotional development, is seeking life advice, including emotionally positive encouragement not unlike that sought by a son of a father.

Conversely, it is problematic that the so called life advice-survival narrative in the film resonates so strongly with young men of color but comes from a script written and produced by White men. Additionally, the film starred a White man who was pretending to be a darker hued Cuban. Equally, these White men lacked any meaningful relationships with ghetto residents, except Pacino's performance as Michael Corleone.

Thus, given the propensity for Black men within hip hop to demand authenticity, *Scarface* should be viewed as inauthentic; however,

Boyz N the Hood, Menace II Society, and *Do the Right Thing* arguably should be the gold standard for an inspired authentic text. Yet, this is not the case. *Scarface* depicts drug dealing and murder as an accepted or respected way of life; so considering who the messengers (filmmakers) are perhaps audience members should reconsider how trustworthy and meaningful the text really is.

Countless films, television programming, music videos, websites, and rap recordings have been inspired by, and heavily referenced homages to, *Scarface*. The names *Scarface* and Tony Montana are interchangeable with gangsta. The chief executive of a major record label uses the name Scarface. Saddam Hussein's money laundering corporation was called Montana Management Company, the name used by the character in the film to launder his drug money. An American foreign policy expert wrote a white paper and used the term "*Scarface* Diplomacy" to describe American aggression in the Middle East. These are good examples of the *Scarface* Effect.

There are, at last count, well over two hundred such films and an undocumented, but known to be substantial, number (in the hundreds) of rap related videos and songs that have been produced—and this product certainly outnumbers the films by a wide margin.[21] A significant new genre, the so named "'Hood" films, which include elements of the *Blaxploitation* genre, has been created due to The *Scarface* Identity in the cinema. This business strategy has ironically resulted in the transfer (by way of ticket sales) of tens of millions of dollars from the poor, who saw themselves represented in these films as mostly negative stereotypes and caricatures against the rich Hollywood infrastructure.[22]

In the final examination what must be understood is that the gangsta agenda, of which *Scarface* has become the most recognizable symbol, was scripted by White males entrenched within the dominant patriarchy that represents Hollywood. It was Pacino, the distinguished White male actor, director De Palma, and especially screenwriter Oliver Stone who captured the imagination of inner city male cinema spectators. This fuse was lit in the midst of an artistic boom by Black males in the 1980s and featured Michael Jackson, Eddie Murphy, and Bill Cosby as the most popular top grossing stars in the music, film, and television industries, respectively. Michael Jackson even tried to stem the oncoming tide of gangsta rap with songs like "Beat It" and "Bad," both of which were baneful antigang anthems. He sold his music, but to the mainstream. At that time hip hop was just a blip on the far distant radar of American culture. Today the gangsta agenda exists as a multi-billion-dollar hyper-commodified goliath—put in play by a few White boys who didn't appear to have a clue as to what they were bequeathing. Are they still clueless? Well, Dr. Dre is a business partner and executive with Apple (he sold his company

Beats Electronics to Apple for $3 billion dollars), Jay-Z has partnered with Samsung on an album release, P. Diddy performed on Broadway, and Snoop Dogg has appeared in commercials for Chrysler—it appears Madison Avenue is drinking the corporate cultural Kool-Aid, and it tastes pretty good (Coward, *The Atlantic*).

NOTES

1. Superstar LeBron James is commonly referred to as "The King," "King James," or the "Chosen One" of the NBA. However, in 2008, *Vogue* magazine decided to choose James for a photo op and take him to another level. James was placed alongside model Gisele Bündchen on the front cover of *Vogue*'s April 2008 publication. James was depicted in a gorilla like pose drawing a comparison to fictional movie monster gorilla King Kong (1933). The controversial cover has received a lot of criticism and continues to fuel the discussion on Black stereotypes in the media (refer to the link for a copy of the photo): www.vogue.com/magazine/article/lebron-james-and-gisele-b252ndchen-dream-team/#1.

2. Camara Jules P. Harrell, *Manichean Psychology: Racism and the Minds of People of African Descent* (Washington, DC: Howard University Press, 1999).

3. Sharon R. Bird, "Welcome to the Men's Club: Homosociality and the Maintenance of Hegemonic Masculinity." *Gender & Society* 10, no. 2 (1996): 120–32.

4. Tommy Lott, *The Invention of Race: Black Culture and the Politics of Representation* (Malden, MA: Blackwell, 1999).

5. Ibid., 123.

6. Cornel West, *Black Popular Culture: A Project by Michelle Wallace*, Gina Dent, ed. (Seattle: Bay Press, 1992), 37.

7. Elijah Anderson, *Code of the Street: Decency, Violence, and the Moral Life of the Inner City* (New York: Norton, 1999).

8. Terry M. Williams, *Crackhouse: Notes from the End of the Line* (Reading, MA: Addison-Wesley, 1992).

9. Clarence Lusane, *Race in the Global Era: African Americans at the Millennium* (Boston: South End Press, 1997).

10. See bell hooks, *Outlaw Culture: Resisting Representations* (New York: Routledge, 1994). Mark Naison is a former sixties radical, who was investigated by the FBI for his membership in the Weatherman organization. He is the author of the bestselling autobiography, *White Boy: A Memoir* (Philadelphia: Temple University Press, 2002).

11. Mark Naison, "Outlaw Culture," *Reconstruction* 1, no. 4 (1994): 128.

12. Charles Mills, *The Racial Contract* (Ithaca: Cornell University Press, 1997). In a groundbreaking study that combined philosophy, sociology, and a razor sharp Marxist critique of capitalism, Mills provided compelling evidence that the failure to implement, the Jeffersonian social contract within the Black population afforded Whites of life, liberty, and the pursuit of happiness was the primary cause of Black social distress. He termed this agreement (or lack thereof) "The Racial Contract." Mills further argued that since slavery was conceived as a means to exploit one race for the benefit of another, the black population as a whole had never been able to "catch up" with whites economically.

13. According to Kevern Verney's *African Americans and U.S. Popular Culture* (New York: Routledge, 2003) hip hop's arrival "reflected the alienation and social and economic deprivation of ghetto communities. Gangsta rappers incorporated images of guns and violence into their lyrics as a mode of artistic self-expression. Their music was rooted in the L.A. street gang culture of the Crips and Bloods and reflected the distrust of any form of authority, most especially White-dominated law enforcement agencies. Straight Outta Compton compared life in the ghetto to the Vietnam War and included a song with the title 'Fuck the Police.' A number of Gangsta lyrics engaged in

revenge fantasies with White law enforcement officers being gunned down by Black ghetto protagonists. Preoccupation with violent early death was another strong theme in Gangsta recordings. Artists frequently fantasized about their own deaths, either in violent shootouts or in executions sanctioned by the state" (95–97).

14. See Douglas G. Glasgow, *The Black Underclass: Poverty, Unemployment, and Entrapment of Ghetto Youth* (San Francisco: Jossey-Bass, 1980), specifically chapter 6, "Adapting to Survival on the Street," 87–104. Glasgow addresses the psychology surrounding both the street hustle and hustler in the chapter, beginning with 1965 in the Watts area of Los Angeles. For the purposes of this study, and with full knowledge that the street behavior Glasgow describes started in America's urban centers decades earlier, the Watts area serves as a useful bookmark for gangsta related psychological profiling since it is commonly known as where the gangsta lifestyle took root and became popular, in part due to the artistic success in promoting the genre through artists such as Tracy "Ice-T" Marrow, and the gangsta rap supergroup N.W.A., which featured militant legends Ice Cube and Easy E.

15. *Monster: The Autobiography of an L.A. Gang Member* by Sanyika Shakur (aka Monster Kody Scott).

16. From Hall, *Representation: Cultural Representations and Signifying Practices*. Hall writes that "producing meaning depends on the practice of interpretation, and interpretation is sustained by us actively using the code-encoding, putting things into the code, and by the person at the other end interpreting or decoding the meaning" (62).

17. "Apparatus," according to film studies theorist Toby Miller, "refers to the interaction between spectators, texts, and technology. Apparatus theory is concerned with the material circumstances of viewing: the nature of filmic projection or video playing, the textual componentry of what is screened, and the psychic mechanisms engaged." Apparatus focuses "on cinema as a 'social machine.' This machine . . . goes into the realm of demands, desires, fantasies, speculation" (Stam and Miller, 402). Miller goes on to write that the power of film as the ultimate device for reality transference is evidenced by its ability, through spectatorship, to "blend narrativity, continuity, point of view, and identification to see spectators become part of the very apparatus designed for them (my emphasis). The apparatus takes the spectatorial illusion of seeming to experience film as real life and makes it a combination of power . . . and engagement" (Ibid). These key observations support my claim that the gangsta identity (in 1983 just at the point of beginning its search for a symbolic entity to represent it) was able to progress in major part because hip hop males within that lifestyle were able to make consistent referrals back to *Scarface*, a text that could not only be replayed over and over but amended to suit the needs of the audience. When DJ Ready Red connected the film to their lifestyle through rap—gangsta had its front man.

18. These events could include a war, as was the case when *Casablanca* was released in 1942 or *Black Hawk Down*, released in January 2002, four months after the attacks on the World Trade Center. Both events affected how audiences looked at the need for patriotism. But audiences also brought into the viewing experience their own feelings about these two events which, according to apparatus theory, would prejudice how they would receive the film. Inner city audiences affected by crime, poverty, gang warfare, and other situations, would bring their feelings about these circumstances into the theater as well.

19. As have been defined within various ethnographic studies, such as those by Anderson, as well as Majors and Billson's study on the inner city survival strategies of young black males and could be utilized as a general explanation for Black male behavior.

20. The audience processes each scene and decodes in accordance with the experiences and values they bring into the viewing, including reality and even dreams. This occurs during each viewing according to the theoretical constructs developed by Hall, Janet Staiger (see *Media Reception Studies* [New York: New York University Press, 2005], 2–8), and Jean-Louis Baudry, whose seminal article, "The Apparatus: Metapsychological Approaches to the Impression of Reality in Cinema," defined the theoretical

change from a purely semiotic approach to reception towards a more psychoanalytical view. Baudry was convinced that cinema created an effect upon the spectator that was accepted as being "more than real." See Baudry's article reproduced in *Film Theory and Criticism*, 690–707.

21. According to imdb.com. See the *Scarface* page on the website at: www.imdb. com/title/tt0086250/movieconnections. As an aside, these inspirations are not unlike what occurs in academia when scholars, out of academic necessity, must reference those icons that have come before them as a means to assert their own validity.

22. These "hood films," for the most part, were not Black independent productions like *Sweet Sweetback* and *Superfly*, but rather major studio productions exploiting the market *Scarface* created. Despite all of the great films produced, directed, and acted by Black filmmakers and movie stars such as Spike Lee, John Singleton, Denzel Washington, Samuel L. Jackson, Jamie Foxx, Forrest Whitaker, and Will Smith, today if you went into any major city ghetto and asked a number of young African American males who is the cinema hero that best represents them today, they would undoubtedly say *Scarface*—Tony Montana. Given all of the heroic fictional deeds seen and enjoyed on the screen in the last twenty-five years, *Scarface* would be an implausible answer.

SIX

Black Popular Culture, *The Boondocks*, and *Black Jesus*

I begin this chapter posing questions regarding what Stuart Hall refers to as "Cultural Politics of Difference" and the "Struggles for Identity," topics often overlooked by members within the Black community. Now, more than ever, with the proliferation of so many voices claiming to represent the essence of Blackness, and considering the assault on Black America by White supremacists, a discussion is needed regarding Black culture. The cultural waters are extremely divided in America, like those divided by God to help the Israelites cross over to dry land:[1]

> Then Moses stretched out his hand over the sea, and all that night the Lord drove the sea back with a strong east wind and turned it into dry land. The waters were divided, and the Israelites went through the sea on dry ground, with a wall of water on their right and on their left. (Exodus 14:21–22)

Communities are split on issues pertaining to social/class status, economic opportunities, education, religion, political ideologies, police brutality and sexuality. Tragically, the politics of the left vs. the right in the United States of America has created a disturbing off-key pitch to the familiar lyrics penned by Francis Scott Key: "For the Land of the Free, and the Home of the Brave."

Moreover, the debate over cultural identity, in particular, has caused many Black Americans to ask the question, how does Blackness (based on an individual's definition) lend itself to the construct of identity? Consideration must be given to the historical perspective of the various forms of representation in popular culture that have been used to construct societal identities. Furthermore, an examination of the distorted images and unclear messages frequently transmitted via the media will help us make

75

some sense of where we (Black folks) have been versus the direction we are heading. According to Stuart Hall:

> [P]opular culture, commodified and stereotyped as it often is, is not at all, as we sometimes think of it, the arena where we find who we really are, the truth of our experience. It is an arena that is profoundly mythic. It is a theater of popular desires, a theater of popular fantasies. It is where we discover and play with the identifications of ourselves, where we are imagined, where we are represented, not only to the audiences out there who do not get the message, but to ourselves for the first time. (Hall, 113)

Hall defines Black popular culture as being a contradictory space—a site of "strategic contestation" similar to so many popular cultures in postmodernity (Hall, 108).

What is the reason for the contradiction? Hall states that it's not from a lack of trying. However, has Black popular culture blended (too much) within the American mainstream? Conversely, the construct of White America's popular culture has always included cultural traditions from the Black repertoire—just ask Elvis Presley.[2] Hall defines Black popular culture as:

> [B]lack popular culture is a contradictory space. It is a site of strategic contestation. But it can never be simplified or explained in terms of the simple binary oppositions that are still habitually used to map it out: high and low; resistance versus incorporation; authentic versus unauthentic; experiential versus formal; opposition versus homogenization. There are always positions to be won in popular culture, but no struggle can capture popular culture itself for our side or theirs. (Hall, 109)

However, the struggle for Black Americans today continues to evolve around a contemptuous depiction of buffoonish images and narratives which are by-products of the past, yet have given way to new constructed nuances (or distinctions) which are often contradictory within the world of Black popular culture. If, as Hall states, cultural strategies should make a difference, how does the artist escape the politics of representation? Do personal experiences (and personal agency) lend to authenticity? Are we making a cultural statement by using the word "Black"? How do we define authenticity and the Black experience? Perhaps the real question becomes: What does being Black really mean, and should it be considered a signifier for the Black community?[3]

Additionally, is there a signifier from a global perspective that addresses the issue of authentic Blackness? Oddly enough, Hall points out that until recently, Western Europe did not have any ethnic disparities. People who lived in Western Europe were considered to be Europeans—end of story. In the United States, however, an interesting debate has emerged amongst people of color (particularly Millennials ages eighteen to thirty-four) regarding the essence of their ethnicity versus the complexion of their skin. Some who consider themselves to be a "person of color" would prefer to be referred to as "American," while others want to be referred to as African American, Asian American, Black American, Hispanic American, and the list goes on.

Conversely, a movement appears to be taking place in the United States by using the term "American" as a way to negate ethnic, cultural, and historical traditions. This homogenous trend to blend is particularly popular with the mainstream, thus creating an opportunity to escape the reality of a contradictory space that is a spin-off of a troubled historical past. According to Stuart Hall, "Cultural hegemony is never about pure victory or pure domination (that's not what the term means); it is never a zero-sum cultural game; it is always about shifting the balance of power in the relations of culture; it is always about changing the dispositions and the configurations of cultural power, not getting out of it" (Hall, 106–107). Hegemony, which is based on the Marxian idea of "superstructure" (i.e., the realm of ideologies, culture, religion, and politics) is the process of enabling an economically and culturally dominant class to retain political power through the manipulation of public opinion. By skillfully handling religion, education, and popular national culture, the ruling class succeeds in having its worldview (i.e., its ideology) generally accepted as tradition or common sense. Therefore, far from being perceived as imposed on people's minds and hearts, hegemonic ideology is met with tacit consent.

Working within the framework of hegemony, Hall deploys the concept of "articulation" to explain the processes of ideological struggle. His use of the term plays on a double meaning to express and connect: on the one hand the process is an articulation, in that meaning has to be expressed in the text; it has to be easy to identify. On the other hand, meaning is always expressed in a specific context (connected to another context, the text could be made to signify something quite different). Thus, the text becomes a site where articulation of multiple meanings can take place. Since texts are multi-accentual, they can be articulated by different people, in different contexts, for different politics. So, meaning becomes a site of negotiation and conflict, an arena where cultural hegemony may be won or lost; an arena where Black Americans have been searching for answers to the racist stereotypes that have haunted them for a very long time (Hall, 108).

Various writers have approached the concept of cultural hegemony from their diverse perspectives. However, no issue is more central to the subject than that of representation. In *The New Cultural Politics of Difference*, Cornel West calls for intellectuals to work within a "new cultural politics of difference" which he sees as an alternative to Eurocentric hegemony, which has dominated cultural and political structures. West writes that the new cultural politics of difference faces three distinct challenges: intellectual, existential, and political. Nonetheless, he gives more weight to the intellectual challenge which centers on the issue of representation. West asserts:

> The modern Black diaspora problematic of invisibility and nameless-
> ness can be understood as the condition of a relative lack of Black
> power to present themselves to themselves and others as complex hu-
> man beings, and thereby contest the bombardment of negative, degrad-
> ing stereotypes put forward by White supremacist ideologies. (West,
> 261)

To counteract these false representations which were based largely on uncontested non-Black norms and models, new representations (images) considered to be morally positive were created to depict homogenous Black communities (as I stated earlier, there appears to be a movement towards a "trend to blend" in America).

However, West suggests that these representations were still framed within Eurocentric hegemonic influences that conformed to non-Black standards of morality. These standards were intended to show that Black people were just like White people, and presumed that all Black people were exactly alike, effectively negating difference based on gender, class, ethnicity, and cultural/historical traditions. Alternatively, authentic voices and images (aesthetically and historically) that express the essence of Blackness are critical components to what Hall considers to be good Black popular culture (A. Nelson).

How critical is freedom of expression to a cultural community? In theory, this linguistic component is very critical to the equalization of cultural representation within a modern world. Perhaps, for *Boondocks* and *Black Jesus* creator Aaron McGruder, the shifting of power (or expression) concerns itself more with the present versus the past. Moreover, McGruder's fictional characters suggest the construct of a Black identity may very well lie in cultural conflicts, misinterpreted voices, and yes, freedom of expression.

HUEY AND RILEY HAVE
A COME TO *BLACK JESUS* MEETING

Not since the early development of the show *South Park* on Comedy Central has there been a more controversial, diverse group of satirical voices than those of the fictional characters created by Aaron McGruder. *The Boondocks*, McGruder's first creation, is based on the original comic strip that he wrote as a student at the University of Maryland. McGruder and his writing associates use the pictorial features of animated charac-ters to touch a nerve on sensitive themes such as racism, Black family structure, sexual orientation, politics, religion, and Black Nationalism. McGruder's characters (in both *The Boondocks* and *Black Jesus*) expose a seemingly, yet unconscious Catch-22 situation for African Americans living as forced émigrés within a White man's society in the twenty-first century. What's more, Aaron McGruder's recurring use of the "N" word has become a common point of discussion amongst youth (regardless of race) within the corridors of many high schools across America that consider themselves fans of the show.

The storyline for *The Boondocks* frequently bridges the gap and juxtaposes taboo subject matter around two central characters: Huey Freeman (who is ten and considered the voice of reason in the show although he reflects the mindset of Malcolm X and Huey Newton) and Riley Freeman (who is eight, militant, and resistant to any type of paternal order). Riley's character (and Huey's) is played by voice actor Regina King. The two young brothers move away from the city of Chicago where they were born, to live with their grandfather Robert Jebediah Freeman in the suburbs; Freeman is also known as "Granddad"(Freeman's character is played by voice actor John Witherspoon). He is also the legal guardian for Riley and Huey. Robert Jebediah Freeman is a firm believer in African American family structure, morals (at times I question what Freeman's morals are really about) and culture. A true patriarch, Robert Jebediah Freeman would be a considered a "Say it Loud I'm Black and I'm Proud" kind of guy. As a father figure in many ways to Riley and Huey, Freeman's character is a counternarrative to so many storylines on television that portray the head of the household in the Black family as a single female who is dependent on food stamps and other forms of government assistance.

Several other characters round out the cast for *The Boondocks*: Tom Dubois (voice actor Cedric Yarbrough) is a lawyer, assistant attorney general, and very affluent. He seems to have a grip on the essence of the "Black Struggle" but is reserved when it comes to controversial issues concerning African Americans—Tom is also a close friend of Robert Freeman and in many ways can be considered another voice of reason in the show. Jazmine DuBois (voice actor Gabby Soleil) is the daughter of Sarah and Tom Dubois. She is often teased by Riley and Huey because of her naïveté and intellect; Sarah Dubois (voice actor Jill Talley) is the wife of Tom Dubois. She is White, liberal, and a civil rights enthusiast. Additionally, she and her husband are members and passionate supporters of the NAACP (National Association for the Advancement of Colored People).[4] Uncle Ruckus (voice actor Gary Anthony Williams) clearly meets the criteria for the stereotype of an "angry Black man." Uncle Ruckus is selective about his acquaintances—especially if they are Black. Uncle Ruckus supports White male Hegemonic influences (in other words, he supports White supremacy) and tries hard to separate himself from the Black community. His character name is a reference to "Uncle Tom" or "Uncle Remus."

Critics have raised their eyebrows at the work of *The Boondocks* creator McGruder repeatedly accusing him of making a mockery of the legacies of Rosa Parks and Dr. Martin Luther King, Jr. In *The Boondocks* episode titled "The Return of King" (season 1, episode 9), the character Riley Freeman displays his lack of knowledge regarding historical information pertaining to Black history at the dinner table when he fails to recognize Dr. Martin Luther King Jr. sitting across from him. Riley's lack of knowledge regarding exactly who King was and the significance of the King legacy prompts him to ask the following questions:

Riley: You don't look famous, what are you, an actor?

Riley: Are you Morgan Freeman?

Robert "Granddad" Freeman: . . . You know that's Martin Luther King . . . now go clear the dishes.

Riley's noncompliant attitude not only opens the door for more probing questions regarding the authenticity of this mysterious man sitting across from him known as "Dr. King"; conversely, it also produces the following reply:

Riley: Why can't this Morgan Freeman dude clear the dishes? Shoot, the Nigga just had a free meal.

Controversial episodic content and storylines such as these have caused critics to question McGruder's insensitivity to civil rights, liberation and the artistic efforts made by BAM (the Black Arts Movement) during the 1960s. Moreover, McGruder's frequent use of the "N-word" (which he does not apologize for) could be considered a bit much, however, an argument can be made that it parallels the patois used in the Blaxploitation films during the 1970s.

Nonetheless, McGruder came under fire in 2006 by Civil Rights activist the Rev. Al Sharpton for his portrayal of Dr. King in "The Return of King" episode. In particular, the setting for the last scene features the Dr. King standing behind the "sacred desk" at the First Grace Church, speaking to several hundred people at a "Martin Luther King Emergency Join the Party Rally." King repeatedly asks the audience members to be quiet by referring to them as "my Brothers and my Sisters" in an effort to bond with the people so that he might say a few words. However, the crowd in attendance which consists mainly of African Americans, ignores King and his plea for silence. The crowd continues their sinful ways by drinking alcohol, fighting with each other (over nothing), and twerking to the beats of hip hop music. The profane actions by the people in attendance (depicted as parishioners within a church fellowship) causes King to utter the following words: "Will you ignorant niggas please shut the hell up." Additionally, King reminds them about his sacrifice for civil rights, by stating: "Is this it? Is this what I got all those ass whippings for?"

The episode aired on January 15, 2006, the day before the national MLK holiday—a day set aside to honor the legacy of Martin Luther King, Jr. What became problematic for many critics are the character choices made by McGruder. Aaron McGruder has a tendency to promote misogynistic themes through the voices/images of his characters. The uncensored sexual hip-hop images of Black women with big butts and breasts (that would require wearing a 38DDD bra) in "The Return of King" episode is an example of what some would consider exploitative and distasteful content. Critics have also called McGruder out for his negative portrayal of King in this episode—King is depicted as a traitor and sympathetic to the terrorist attacks that occurred on 9/11. In one particular scene, King is asked a question on the TV program *Politically Incorrect*: what should the United States's response be to the attacks on 9/11? King responded by saying: "Well . . . as a Christian, we are taught that you should love thy enemy and turn the other cheek." Martin Luther King was frequently criticized for his nonviolent views (most notably by Malcolm X in his speech to the Northern Grass Roots Leadership Conference titled "Message to the Grass Roots" on November 10, 1963, in Detroit, Michigan). Malcolm X told audience members:

> So I cite these various revolutions brothers and sisters to show you, you don't have a peaceful revolution. You don't have a turn the other cheek revolution, there is no such thing as a nonviolent revolution. Only kind of revolution that's nonviolent is the Negro Revolution. The only revolution based on loving your enemy is the Negro revolution. . . . That's no revolution. ("Message to the Grass Roots")

Equally, King's nonviolent message is (through the narrative) rejected by McGruder as well.

During a 2006 interview on ABC *Nightline*, Aaron McGruder questions whether or not his (King's) character would work in a modern context. Apparently, McGruder has concerns on whether King's rhetorical messages would cut the grade in today's society. Alternatively, according to McGruder, Dr. King's final speech in this episode was one of frustration; thus the reason for his excessive use of the word "Nigga." McGruder is unapologetic for the use of the words "Nigga" and "Nigger" as part of his narratives. He states that "On his show, we don't use the N-Word; we say Nigga" (ABC *Nightline*, 2006).

The episode ends with King—tired, angry, and frustrated—making the comment, "I will not get there with you . . . I'm going to Canada" (the King speech also provoked a second civil rights revolution at the end of the show). King's movement to another country, for me, is similar to Dr. W. E. B. Du Bois's move to Ghana in 1961. Frustrated with racism in the United States, Dubois left for Ghana in 1961 and ultimately became a citizen in 1963. There appear to be no hidden agendas within the text of *The Boondocks* that need to be decoded; his characters tell it like it is.

Regardless of how one decodes or dissects the message, McGruder's "in your face" approach forces the spectator to closely examine the subject matter for diverse interpretations that may offer a deeper meaning, ultimately causing the viewer to question issues of social identity, class status and race relations in America.

For satirist Aaron McGruder, controversy continues to follow the trail of his politically incorrect messages. Shortly after he (some say involuntarily) gave up the ghost to his creative control of *The Boondocks* to Sony Pictures in 2014, his satirical voice has been resurrected in a new show entitled *Black Jesus* which premiered on August 7, 2014, on the Cartoon Network (Adult Swim). The premise of the show (the creators are Aaron McGruder and Mike Clattenburg) focuses on a man who calls himself Jesus and believes that he is Jesus (Jesus is played by Gerald "Slink" Johnson). Black Jesus lives and sleeps (wherever he can) on the Southwest side of Compton. He doesn't work, smokes reefer, and drinks cheap beer that he turns into fine yak (commonly referred to as Cognac or Brandy); however, he is concerned about the sick, the oppressed, and strongly believes in loving thy neighbor as thyself—brotherly love is key. Jesus would be considered the protagonist and voice of reason in the show.

The rest of Jesus' disciples and adversaries (cast members) include the following: Vic (the antagonist) is the apartment building manager who thinks Jesus is a con man and is determined to bring Jesus down. Vic's persona (played by Charlie Murphy) has traits similar to the Pharisees in the Bible. Lloyd (played by John Witherspoon) is a drunken snitch willing to do anything for food, water, shelter, alcohol, and money. Vic pays Lloyd to spy and keep close tabs on Jesus for him. However, most of the time Floyd is too drunk to complete the tasks. Maggie (played by Kali Hawk) is part of Jesus' inner circle. She is somewhat rebellious, yet she appears to be committed to the cause and close to Jesus (similar to the relationship Mary Magdalene had with Jesus in the Bible). Ms. Tudi (played by Angela E. Gibbs) is a single parent who is financially stable; however, she is always looking for her next hustle. Ms. Tudi enjoys selling marijuana (for profit) and often refers to her son Boonie as a "fat, bad luck lazy nigga like your father"—ironically, bad luck appears to be Ms. Tudi's ruptured Achilles tendon during the first season. Boonie (played by Corey Holcomb) is a momma's boy who doesn't work, but enjoys smoking his mother's product and wasting her profits. Boonie is also part of the inner circle and has a close relationship with Jesus. Jason (played by Antwon Tannor) is torn between his friendship with Jesus, the disciples, and his atheist cop girlfriend Diane. He is constantly pressured by the inner circle to do the right thing, which is contrary to what his girlfriend wants him to do. Fish (played by Andra Fuller) is a hot head, impatient supporter of Jesus. Fish is another member of Jesus' inner circle and his character traits are similar to those of the biblical Peter from the

New Testament. Two other characters round out the cast: Diane, the atheist Compton cop (played by Valenzia Algrin) and Trayvon (played by Andrew Bachelor)—Trayvon is the youngest member of Black Jesus' inner circle.

The project (located in the projects of Compton) of building a community garden is a critical component to the ministry work Jesus feels compelled to do. He is driven by the possibility/opportunity of planting a garden in the hood (perhaps a biblical reference to "The Garden of Gethsemane") that would include vegetables and weed (not the lawn weeds that choke out more desirable plants). His determination for the garden to become a reality juxtaposes several other controversial popular culture depictions of Jesus, which include a White hippie in San Francisco (during the Jesus Movement in the 1960s); Andrew Lloyd Webber and Tim Rice's Jesus in the 1970 rock opera/rock musical *Jesus Christ Superstar;* Martin Scorsese's film adaptation *The Last Temptation of Christ* (1988); J. J.'s painting of a Black Jesus in the Evan's family home (*Good Times,* 1974); *Jesus Christ Vampire Hunter* (2001), a campy cult film that focuses on Jesus' present-day struggle to safeguard lesbians of Ottawa, Ontario, Canada, from vampires. Mel Gibson's *The Passion of the Christ* (2004); "Jesus Walks," a song from Kanye West's 2004 debut album *The College Dropout;* and the iconic image of the gothic cross on the back of Tupac Shakur (many within the hip hop community refer to Tupac as the Black Jesus).

According to Princeton Theological Seminary Associate Professor Rev. Dr. Yolanda Pierce:

> The show raises some important theological questions. "If Jesus were to return, what would Jesus look like?" . . . "What would Jesus do? And would we, those people who consider themselves as Christians, as I do, recognize Jesus if the historical Jesus is not the blond-haired, blue-eyed [man] of our usual stained-glass depictions?" (NPR, August 2004)

Moreover, Pierce's comment draws a parallel to the biblical Jesus who eats with tax collectors and sinners, yet was criticized for his association with the unrighteous (Mark. 2.16). Pierce maintains:

> The provocative setting—a Jesus who drinks 40s, curses and smokes weed—might also reflect the reality of people who could use some ministering. "Especially people at the margins, who may be using weed or who may be drinking as a way to soften the brutality of their everyday existence" . . . Jesus would preach to those whom Scripture calls "the least of these." (NPR, August, 2004)

However, the fuss isn't necessarily over what Black Jesus would do, but the language used by Jesus and his disciples.

Before the show premiered, several churches and conservative religious organizations consider the satirical content in *Black Jesus* to be not only offensive but also impious. Conservative Christian activists, led by the group One Million Moms and the American Family Association, are pushing Cartoon Network's Adult Swim series to cancel the show *Black Jesus*, which they call offensive and "full of lies." Monica Cole, the director of One Million Moms, stated "the show is 'blasphemous, irreverent and disrespectful.'" However, Ms. Cole's comments were based on the trailer (she had not seen a full episode when she made her remarks).

Kerry Burkey, who is the senior pastor at the Rockledge Church of Christ in Compton, California, sees the show as a "symbol of a decline in American pop culture." Pastor Burkey showed the *Black Jesus* trailer to several youth at his church, and states: "It was horrible, disgusting and completely offensive. Down to a person, everyone in the youth group was offended. It just shows where we are as a nation. . . . We have no respect for God" (*USA Today*, August 2014).

Here are a few comments from three of my students that took a course with me at The State University of New York at Oswego (SUNY Oswego) titled *Hip Hop in Cinema & TV*:

> There was almost a lack of a storyline in the first episode of *Black Jesus*. It was more of an introduction and a day in the life of Black Jesus. He met up with a few of his friends who asked him to help them pick up "a brick" of marijuana for one of their mothers. They eventually did so and got jumped. They ran after the criminals and got their money and the marijuana but Jesus was arrested. He got out of it (because he's Jesus) and went back to his friends who surprised him by setting up a garden that Jesus had been saying he wanted to create. All in all the show was very entertaining and I liked the way that the creators of the show paired Jesus with characters and situations the average person wouldn't expect him to be with or in. It made me ask questions, morally and socially. Jesus and his friends were the main characters in the show. (Robert Dezendorf, student, SUNY Oswego)

Another student remarked:

> It is hard for the characters in the show [*Black Jesus*] to always do the right thing when other people do not have Jesus guiding them to stay on track to do the right thing. In this show the characters also say the "N" word to each other and curse regularly throughout the show and even Black Jesus curses. (Keith Mirra, student, SUNY Oswego)

Emily Santos commented:

> I heard the commotion of *Black Jesus* and people getting mad because "Jesus isn't black." I saw the first episode, "Smokin', Drinkin, and Chillin." The episode focused around the characters of Jesus and his friends Boonie, Jason and Fish. It was a really funny show that made me have to pause a few times and write down the funny quips. Like when the drug dealers who tricked the group were actually white guys and Jesus said "Michael, Chandler, Ross!" and then tells them how their mother would be mad if they weren't at water polo practice instead. There were of course plenty of stereotypes of black people (as CNN's Don Lemon would also agree), such as them smoking weed, breaking rules,

and being "lazy." In one scene, Jesus is being arrested and the cop says, "stop resisting," while Jesus has his hands up. Another thing that was funny was that Jesus was listing all the things he needed for the barbecue and Trayvon asked how he was going to get the supplies without money. Jesus replies, "All you need is the holy spirit." I thought that was hilarious since people think that just praying will help and God/ Jesus will fix everything. I'm most likely going to watch the rest of the season. (Emily Santos, student, SUNY Oswego)

McGruder's writing style allows the viewer to consider varied readings that question issues of societal uniqueness, class distinction and race relations in America. Writers/Producers such as Aaron McGruder; Trey Parker and Matt Stone (*South Park*); Dave Chappelle (*Chappelle's Show*); and Matt Groening (*The Simpsons*) use parody to make political and social commentary. It's that simple. Whether you agree or disagree with the content—that's their intentions.

In the end, is it such a bad thing to see depictions on television of militant youth who repeatedly use the word "Nigga" and other homophobic comments? Alternatively, how about a Black man who is basically homeless in the hood, hangs with his homies on the streets, smokes weed, drinks cognac, performs a few miracles from time to time, and professes to be Jesus? Perhaps, God is the only one who can answer the question regarding the disservice to the Black community stereotypical roles have played throughout the history of film and TV. Conversely, when you see Jesus cursing, you know that you have problems in society. However, considering the racial divide in this country at the present time, maybe He needs to.

> I don't think the way you think. The way you work isn't the way I work.
>
> —Isaiah 55:8 (*The Message*)

NOTES

1. The reference is in regard to the oppressive situation the Israelites were in.

2. The Black repertoire, according to Hall, consists of three performance spaces (or forms of expression) that have been linked to the creation of Black representation and identity. The three performance spaces are: style, music, and the role of the body and its significance to representation (Hall, 27). Elvis Presley has been considered by many to be a thief. His musical efforts and dance movements often mimicked the talents of Black performers such as Little Richard, Chuck Berry, and Otis Blackwell. From their lyrics "Fight the Power" Public Enemy states that "Elvis was a hero to most but he never meant shit to me you see straight up racist that sucker was simple and plain motherfuck him and John Wayne."

3. Oddly, Hall points out until recently, Western Europe did not have any ethnicities. People who lived in Western Europe were considered to be Europeans, end of story. However, in the United States an interesting debate has developed between people of color and White America. Some persons of color just want to be referred to as "American." Others want to be referred to as African American, Black American,

Hispanic American, the list goes on. What I find problematic is that Whites in the United States use the term "American" as a tool to negate ethnic cultural/historical traditions.

4. Founded in 1909, the NAACP is the nation's oldest and largest civil rights organization. From the ballot box to the classroom, the thousands of dedicated workers, organizers, leaders and members who make up the NAACP continue to fight for social justice for all Americans (www.naacp.org/).

SEVEN

American Culture and the Black Situation Comedy

He will fill your mouth with laughter, your lips will spill over into cries of delight.

—Job 8:21 (*The Voice*)

My purpose for writing this chapter is not to reprocess or rehash information on a subject that has already been thoroughly researched by other scholars (I will reference the work of some of those scholars throughout this chapter). Quite frankly, I had no intentions of writing this until a reviewer for the manuscript suggested I write a chapter on Black situation comedies and Black humor—so I decided to write something. I began to ask myself questions about the subject matter such as: What views have already been expressed by other scholars? What has or has not already been argued? How can I introduce something new regarding Black humor and the genre—Black situation comedy? I decided that a good starting point would be to reflect on my own experiences (personally and professionally).

While sound scholarship makes and supports arguments on the basis of theoretic frameworks or analytical procedures, many times personal experiences that support a particular interpretation of the available specifics or information are absent from the discussion. On one hand, my work in education has caused me to defer judgment when new arguments, information, and evidence on a particular issue or subject matter are presented. In contrast, working as a practitioner in the entertainment industry has given me an opportunity to re-evaluate and reflect upon the historical baggage that has often been associated with media negativity and stereotyping—the quest to create a positive identity continues to be a daunting task for Black actors, Black audience members, and Black

Americans living within an inequitable society. We (as spectators) have been forced to witness the racist "spectacle" on stage, on film, and on television for quite some time—the journey hasn't been easy. Since we live in a society which places a value on the spectacle, what are the consequences for living in an image based culture? I would suggest the appearance (visual) supports the spectacle. However, when and where does the "spectacle" end?

For several decades White America's awareness and obsession with Black culture came from theatrical performances of dance, music, and comedic skits performed by Whites in Blackface—these theatrical performances became known as "the minstrel show" or minstrelsy (in chapter 4 I reference the work of scholar Eric Lott and his research on the practices of Blackface as a performative "spectacle" and the various aspects of minstrelsy). Minstrel shows were founded on the comic enactment of racial stereotypes and included the imitation of Black music, dance, and speaking in what was considered a plantation dialect spoken by slaves. Considered the most popular form of entertainment in America at one point, minstrel shows featured a variety of jests, songs, dances, and parodies based on disturbing stereotypes of African American slaves. The minstrel show performers (many of whom were White) would blacken their faces with charcoal paste or burnt cork (thus the term "Black face") and would dance a buffoonish jig while singing the lyrics to a song ("Jump Jim Crow") that went something like this:

> Weel about and turn about and do jis so,
> Eb'ry time I weel about I jump Jim Crow

Because of the popularity of these shows, African Americans were eventually branded as lazy, irresponsible Coons. Other labels or character names associated with minstrel performances were "Darkies," "Mammies," "Picaninny," and "Sambo," all of which served as a comic relief for the White spectators of these performances.

Additionally the influence of minstrelsy was evident in vaudeville, radio, and television as well as in the American film and music industry. These offensive performances of minstrelsy motivated Frederick Douglass to make the following statements in a newspaper article published by *The North Star*: "…the filthy scum of white society, who have stolen from us a complexion denied to them by nature, in which to make money, and pander to the corrupt taste of their white fellow-citizens" (*The North Star*, October 1848). Douglass spoke out against the disingenuous appropriation (and exploitation) of Black culture as well as the use of racist ideology for the purposes of capital gain and entertainment. Ironically, I would question if a similar scenario is being played out today with shows such as *black*-ish (ABC) and *Empire* (FOX) as well as *Fresh off the Boat* (ABC) and *Dr. Ken* (ABC); the latter two play off Asian stereotypes. Critics have argued the character depictions in all four shows promote images that many consider to be demeaning and damaging to the progression of a positive self-identity for both Asian and Black Americans.

The topic of Black Americans in situation comedies provides for some attention-grabbing questions along with many contentious interpretations of the various characters Black actors have played through the years. Historically, Black images in comedic situations on the small screen dates back to the beginning of television. During the early days, Black performers were often spotlighted at the local and network level. However, the themes of these television programs repeatedly presented disturbing images of African American culture; regrettably, many early small screen programs portrayed Black characters in demeaning, stereotypical roles which was not much different from the minstrel shows during the nineteenth century.

SO, WHAT IS A BLACK SITCOM?

"How you like one cross your lip?"(Fred Sanford, *Sanford and Son*). Black situation comedies can be defined as comedic situations with recurring cast members who are people of African origin, the principal characters in particular (Nelson, 79). In many cases, the storylines focus on the Black family structure and the struggles associated with Black family life. Black sitcoms attempt to show a particular perspective of Black American lifestyles, principles, ethics, standards, and views. Although sitcoms with primarily Black characters have been present since the earliest days of network television (there were also the early radio program sitcoms *Beulah* and *Amos 'n' Andy*) this genre rose to prominence in the 1990s.

According to Bowling Green State University Associate Professor Angela Nelson, Black situation comedies can be broken down into three types: *domcoms* (which are referred to as domestic comedies), *actcoms* (action comedies), and *dramedies* (dramatic comedies) (79).[1] Similar to American situation comedies, much of the action takes place in the home, at work, combined home/work situations (ABC TV's *black*-ish is an example of this) or in other settings such as on college campuses or military bases (Nelson, 80). Principal characters have very little, if any interaction with other ethnic groups. Additionally, Nelson states that

> Black sitcoms are not "Black" in that they exhibit an African worldview of Black philosophy of life. Rather, they are Black because the performers are Black, and their characters are supposedly dealing with their sitcom situations from a "Black" perspective. This is seen clearly when issues or concerns that are unique to African American life, history, and culture are explored including such issues as racism and discrimination. (80)

Yet, according to Nelson, "they are unsuccessful for the most part because the sitcom formula itself is too rigid to allow such originality and creativity" (80). Black sitcoms often illustrate inaccurate or unrealistic portrayals of Blacks (especially narratives pertaining to the Black family), harmful stereotypes associated with buffoonish images of Blacks, and very little, if any aesthetic value—the historical presence of Black sitcoms on commercial television dates back sixty-plus years (1948–present).

What are stereotypes? Are stereotypes always negative? Are some positive? By definition, a stereotype can be considered a belief that all people with similar characteristics are the same—stereotypes are used to present oversimplified perceptions (or images) of individuals. Stereotypes are also used to categorize a group of people (e.g., Islam is a dangerous religion and all Muslims are Jihadists). As audience members, we have allowed ignorance to factor in on our personal perceptions of people with other cultures; thus using those preconceived notions as justification to dislike or "hate" another person or group of people has created a divisive climate in America. Does the promotion of Black stereotype images (which are often depicted in Black situation comedies) do more harm than good with respect to the progression of the cultural contributions by Black Americans in American Culture? To that point, according to Dr. Angela Nelson, traditionally Black stereotypes

> were used to symbolize racial differences between whites and blacks in order to maintain the inferior status of African Americans, to show that blacks differed significantly from whites "physically, intellectually, and temperamentally," to prove that animosity between whites and blacks was inevitable, to show that miscegenation—sexual relations between people of different races, especially of different skin colors, leading to the birth of children—was a "sublime evil," and to demonstrate that a biracial society was an impossibility best remedied by the outright removal of African Americans from United States territory or through various forms of subordination to the dominant white society. (185)

Similar to the past, today's shows (which predominantly feature all Black cast members) still use storylines that have a tendency to foster images of buffoonery (the character J. J. from *Good Times*, 1972–1979 and *Martin*, 1992–1997 fall in this category), coonery (*Meet the Browns*, 2009–2012), thuggery (*Empire*, 2015 although not a Black sitcom is still an example of this), and minstrelsy. The visuals (and symbols) associated with the depiction of Black stereotypes has become commonplace in film and television thus creating a "Black iconography" that has resulted in White America developing preconceived notions regarding Black culture.

Nelson places the representation of Black Americans (character types) in Black sitcoms into four categories of cultural communal discourse that reflect upon the racial attitudes in America regarding social distance and stereotyping:

1. *Hybrid Minstrelsy and Black Employment, 1948–1965*: Black characters in this period mimic some of their audible and derogatory imagery from White minstrel humor (examples would include burnt-cork makeup, coonery gestures, and mammy caricatures).

2. *Assimilationist Minstrelsy and Black Glamour, 1961–1973*: The Assimilationist Minstrelsy and Black Glamour Period refers to Black characterizations that reflect upon any of the issues pertaining to race, class, and gender conflicts that occurred in America during the 1960s. Throughout this period, Black character portrayals made little reference (if any) to Black culture in their appearance or behaviors—these Black images appeared for the most part to have fully integrated into the conventional American way of life (Nelson, 196).

3. *Assimilated Hybrid Minstrelsy, 1972–1983*: "Assimilated Hybrid Minstrelsy refers to Norman Lear and Bud Yorkin's (re)creation of black buffoonish characters" (Nelson, 197). Most Black sitcoms during this period embraced the language and culture of White America while exhibiting characteristics of Black Nationalism (Nelson, 197).

4. *Multiculturalism, Simultaneity, and Diversification, 1984—Present*: It was during this period that the comedic roles for African Americans increased significantly on television. Comedic relief and storylines (in terms of performance from Black cast members) focused heavily on a Black vernacular as a way of expression versus the shuck and jive minstrelsy of the past (Nelson, 200). Several Black sitcom series relied heavily on what is referred to as Black English or "Ebonics" as a form of verbal expression. In particular, the sitcom *Martin* (Martin is played by Martin Lawrence) had a tendency to deliver phrases such as "ass-whoopin"; "Bruh-Man"; Get to steppin'! Step!"; and "WAZZUP!"

THE SIX HISTORICAL ERAS OF BLACK SITUATION COMEDY

Taking it a step further, in her book *African American Viewers and the Black Situation Comedy: Situating Racial Humor*, scholar Robin R. Means Coleman cites the work of Nelson and suggests that Black situation comedies on network television can be broken down into six historical categories:[2]

1. *TV Minstrelsy (1950–1953)*: A period of ridicule, Blacks were depicted as comical, inept, second class citizens operating for the amusement of Whites. The Black nuclear family (when there was representation written within the storyline) was often portrayed as dysfunctional (e.g., *Amos 'n' Andy*, 1951–1953).

2. *Nonrecognition (1954–1967)*: The Nonrecognition Era reflects the disappearance of Black situation comedies on network television

after the cancellation of *Beulah* (1950–1953) and *Amos 'n' Andy* (1951–1953). According to Means Coleman, during this period Black sitcoms took a back seat to bus boycotts, civil unrest, church bombings, marches, and the use of high pressure water hoses and dogs by police on unprotected demonstrators.

3. *Assimilationist (1968–1971)*: Mainstream conformity is key during this period. Subject matter regarding Black culture and the essence of Blackness is ignored (the essence of Blackness and the phrase "Black is Beautiful" was made popular during the Black Power Movement during the 1960s and 1970s). The assimilationist discourse is characterized by a rejection to any conversations pertaining to Black sociopolitical struggles, Black pride, and Black identity. The sitcom *Julia* starring Diahann Carroll (1968–1971) is an example of one of the first assimilationist shows.

4. *The Lear Era: Ridiculed Black Subjectivity and Social Relevancy (1972–1983)*: According to Means Coleman, Norman Lear was innovated in that his comedies confronted many of the racial issues and reflected the racial consciousness among African American people during the 1970s and 1980s. Lear's social commentary, infused within the storylines of his shows, frequently touched on issues pertaining to race, racism, class, communal economic problems and other cultural disparities. The popularity of shows such as *The Jeffersons, Good Times*, and *Sanford and Son* marked a new era of representation for African Americans on TV. However, as Means Coleman and Nelson both point out, Norman Lear failed to assign any relevancy or worth to Black culture (93). The choices made by his characters (agency) are questionable and Lear has been criticized for his character portrayals of buffoonery (J. J. on *Good Times*); minstrelsy-based characters (Bubba and Grady on *Sanford and Sons*); and the "mammy" (Florida Evans in *Good Times*).

5. *The Cosby Era: Diversity and Family (1984–1989)*: The Cosby Era (thanks in large part to *The Cosby Show*) increased Black situation comedy programming; and improved the images of Black family structure—*The Cosby Show* set the standard for non-ridicule, celebrated Black culture, and presented African Americans in a positive light. "*The Cosby Show* depicted an assimilated upper-class African American traditional family that was absent of any dysfunction, deviance, or deficiency" (Means Coleman, 95). For the first time on television America witnessed a Black nuclear family that included a working professional couple living in the same household.

6. *Neo-Minstrelsy (1990–present)*: According to Means Coleman, the Neo-Minstrelsy Era is defined by its "Sambo, coon, prized criminal character types" (104). Means Coleman also states that "Neo-Minstrelsy, as a term, describes the full circle that Black situation come-

dy has come in its treatment of Blackness, explicitly acknowledging a renewed emphasis on the ridicule and the subordination of Black culture as homogeneously deviant" (104–105).

SO, WHAT HAS CHANGED?

Is there a renewed interest in storylines that focus on Black issues, Black lives, and the Black family on network TV? Or has Father Time caught up with the Huxtables? Has the scenery changed much for the Evans family in Chi-Raq (Chicago) and for other African Americans living in urban areas across America? After all, Oprah Winfrey passed up George Jefferson some time ago en route to the eastside and that deluxe apartment in the sky. Conversely, Black people are still struggling trying to make ends meet the same way Fred Sanford did working as a junk dealer while living in the Watts neighborhood of South Central L.A. I guess the question becomes: Will African Americans ever really own a slice of the pie?

Going forward, perhaps the complexity and progression of Black America on television should focus on storylines and character roles that don't depend upon controversial situations in order to "sell the message." According to film scholar and historian J. Fred Macdonald:

> The problem confronting African Americans, however, is more complex. Given the historic intolerance of the dominant culture in the United States, it seems myopic and even dangerous for blacks to tolerate portrayals of themselves that are not complimentary. For all their achievements and honors, black Americans are still struggling for social empowerment, still seeking to integrate the entrenched and obstinate white power structure. Thus, depictions that might connote generic inequality—be it physical, intellectual, social, political, or otherwise—have dire implications that affect individuals as well as the entire race. (281–82)

Maybe a sitcom on network TV about a forty-something successful African American male who has a great job, a stunning biracial wife, and four beautiful kids could discredit some of the age old negative depictions of African Americans—it could just be what ABC's fictional doctor, Richard Webber (*Grey's Anatomy*), ordered. After all, America preaches and promotes multicultural ideologies, policies, cultural diversity, and advocates for equal respect to the various cultures in society. Regardless of ethnicity, religious beliefs, or sexual preferences, cultural tolerance has become the new buzz word in the twenty-first century.

So what was ABC thinking when they decided to add a show titled *black*-ish to their Wednesday night Primetime line-up? Critics have questioned if the title supports (or hurts) the many voices heard, and accomplishments made during the Civil Rights Movement. Does the title just reinforce the debated topic of buffoonery and coon like images often associated with roles played by Black actors in situation comedies? Or does it suggest something different?

I would argue television has entered into an era of reconciliation. Storylines for Black sitcoms on network television present a conciliatory—non-assimilation approach to Black family life. It's a period where the Black experience (or for that matter, any cultural experience) is the focus of family structure. Although family patriarchs lecture on history and traditions, Black youth are determined and feel pressured to "fit in" because of cultural isolation and confusion over personal identity (am I really Black?)—participation equates to assimilation. Thus the trade-off for adolescent characters on Black situation comedies is selective hearing toward family history and traditions; additionally, Mom and Dad question their decision to raise a family in a suburb flowing with "milk and honey," community festivals, malls, and Starbucks.[3] (A similar prototype exists for adolescent characters in the show *Fresh off the Boat* on ABC.)

I have to admit, I was not a fan of the title *black*-ish. I grew up watching Black situation comedies such as *Julia*, *Sanford and Son*, *Good Times*, and *The Jeffersons*. These shows spoke to the spirit of my Black experience (to be honest, at age fifteen, I don't think I fully grasped the concept of the Black experience). The titles really never identified a particular Black person or group of Black people per say (with the exception of *Julia*—in this case the title reflected who the principle character was in the show; I guess an argument could be made for *The Jeffersons* as well). What the titles did allow audience members to do was enter into the life of a young African American woman working as a nurse who is a widow and trying to raise a young son alone (*Julia*, 1968–1971); reflect upon a father-son relationship that was committed to loving one another regardless of how frustrated they were with each other (*Sanford and Son*, 1972–1977); witness a poverty-stricken Black family trying to make do with what they had living in the projects of Chicago (*Good Times*, 1974–1979); and share the conversations of a bigoted Black entrepreneur (George Jefferson) and his family who recently become rich, and are not shy about how they spend their money—they firmly believe they are living the "American Dream" (*The Jeffersons*, 1975–1985). Maybe the goal is not to be politically correct. Regardless of all the objections to the *black*-ish title (Donald Trump was the show's strongest critic, calling the title "racist") *black*-ish has become a hit for ABC. For now, creator Kenya Barris' family sitcom continues its journey of success down the road of Black experience (Kenya Barris recently signed a multiyear deal with ABC Studios for *black*-ish).

The show *black*-ish focuses on Andre "Dre" Johnson (played by Anthony Anderson). "Dre considers himself the family patriarch and when he looks at his life—he sees a beautiful wife and four kids living happily in their colonial home in the 'burbs" (abc.go.com). However, are there consequences for success? In Dre's mind, success has led to the loss of cultural identity and individuality. Dre Johnson is concerned that the commitment to achieve success has created a sense of assimilation for his family. Old school in a lot of ways, he views the world from a different perspective than his family.

His wife, named Rainbow (also referred to as "Bow" played by Tracee Ellis Ross) is a successful anesthesiologist. She is liberal, attractive, and biracial; she doesn't always agree with the viewpoints of her man, but they are determined to give their children a better life versus what they had. She is encouraged by Dre's determination and drive to become the first Black senior executive at his ad firm."With a little help from his dad (Pops), Dre sets out to establish a sense of cultural identity for his family that honors their past while embracing the future" (abc.go.com).

Rainbow Johnson believes in a "societal rainbow of equality"—a society that is colorless. However, Dre has a tendency to question her Blackness (because she is biracial) which at times, blurs the color lines and suggests a sense of double consciousness—something W. E. B. Du Bois addressed in his book *The Souls of Black Folk* (1903). The term which was coined by Du Bois speaks to issues concerning the Black experience and a divided identity in America; in his writing, Du Bois often commented on the challenges of being Black and living in a Eurocentric society.

The rest of the cast for *black*-ish includes Zoey Johnson (played by Yara Shahidi). Zoey is fifteen, pretty, witty and is quite popular in school. However, she is focused on "The Material World"; Zoey exhibits a sense of privilege and is a child content with unearned entitlements. Andre Jr. (often referred to as Junior) is played by Marcus Scribner. Similar to Zoey, Andre (who prefers to be called Andy) is trying to make sense of the complexities of growing up in an assimilated and privileged environment. He respects the stories of old regarding the Black experience told by his father (Dre) and especially his grandfather (Pops). Yet, Andy would prefer to play on the school's field hockey team versus playing the Black man's game of basketball. Andy likes what he has and enjoys living in White suburbia. Other cast members include Diane Johnson (played by Marsai Martin) and Jack Johnson (played by Miles Brown). Diane and Jack are the Johnson family's six-year-old twins—both children are extremely gifted and talented; Ruby Johnson (Dre's mother—played by Jenifer Lewis) and Pops Johnson (Dre's father—played by Laurence Fishburne) round out the rest of the cast. Fishburne is also the executive producer for the series.

MOVIN' ON UP/THE CULTURAL DEBATE

The late film scholar and historian J. Fred MacDonald in his book *Blacks and White TV: African Americans in Television Since 1948* suggests the increased visibility of African Americans on television has produced a mixed blessing. Although the growth of Black talent on the small screen has enhanced the careers of a number of performers, according to Mac-Donald, television has created a sense of cultural and social assimilation for the Black middle class. MacDonald suggests that today's storylines, which feature all Black cast members, no longer "display the authentic qualities that make African Americans distinct." Furthermore MacDonald asserts that "Blacks on TV usually exhibit the bourgeois values, habits, and attitudes that are so familiar in White characterization" (279).

Maybe shows like *black*-ish are headed in the right direction by debunking issues of assimilation while at the same time creating positive images (representation) for minorities on television—network television has really never been sensitive to the cultural needs of African Americans; perhaps that has changed. As the theme lyrics from the show *The Jeffersons* points out: "We finally got a piece of the pie." The sad commentary for most Black Americans is someone ate the entire pie a long time ago.

INFLUENTIAL BLACK SITCOMS AND VARIETY SHOWS (1950–PRESENT)

Rankings are based on early years to present (criteria is centered on historical significance, writing, character roles, cultural impact, contributions to American society, and my personal opinions).[4]

1. *Beulah* (1950–1953) is not considered a Black situation comedy, however the central themes concentrated on family matters; the key character role was an African American domestic female worker named Beulah (played by Ethel Waters and Louis Beavers). Her wit and wisdom was often seen as a "voice of reason" during the run of the series.
2. *Amos 'n' Andy* (1951–1953) was based off the radio comedy "Amos 'n' Andy" (1920s–1950s). Stories mostly centered on The Kingfish's schemes to get rich, often by duping his brothers in the Mystic Knights of the Sea Lodge.
3. *The Nat King Cole Show* (1956–1957) was, according to film scholar/historian J. Fred MacDonald, "By any standard, *The Nat King Cole Show* was top-flight entertainment. Cole smoothly hosted this showcase for his musical talents. He sang his famous ballads and played piano in front of a first-rate orchestra. Sometimes, too, he exhibited the jazz dexterity that made him famous in the first place." Unsuccessful at reaching a mass audience and combined with poor ratings (the show was playing opposite *Robin Hood* on CBS which was one of the top-rated shows on TV), *The Nat King Cole Show* suffered from not having a consistent national sponsor. Although Cole was talented as a host for the musical variety show on NBC, the show had a short run.

4. *Julia* (1968–1971) is notable for being one of the first weekly sitcom series to depict an African American woman in a non-stereotypical role. Previous television series featured African American lead characters, but the characters were usually portrayed in domestic/servant roles. The show stars actress and singer Diahann Carroll, and aired on NBC from 1968 to 1971.

5. *The Bill Cosby Show* (1969–1971) aired for two seasons on NBC from 1969 until 1971; the show was sponsored by Procter & Gamble. It marked Bill Cosby's return to television in a starring role after co-starring with Robert Culp in *I Spy*.

6. *The Flip Wilson Show* (1970–1974) was an hour-long variety show that aired in the United States on NBC from 1970 to 1974. The show starred comedian Flip Wilson and was one of the first American television programs starring a Black person in the title role to become highly successful with a White audience. Specifically, it was the first successful network variety series starring an African American. During its first two seasons, it was one of the highest rated Nielsen programs on network television. (Nielsen is a global leader in consumer measurement. The Nielsen ratings are based on methodology driven by electronic meters and diaries that measure audience engagement—Nielson.com.)

7. *Fat Albert and the Cosby Kids* (1972–) is an animated series created, produced, and hosted (in live action bookends) by comedian Bill Cosby, who also lent his voice to a number of characters, including Fat Albert himself. The show premiered in 1972 and ran until 1985. The show, based on Cosby's remembrances of his childhood gang, centered on Albert (known for his catchphrase "Hey hey hey!") and his friends.

8. *Sanford and Son* (1972–1975) aired on the NBC television network from 1972 to 1975. The star of the show was the great comedic actor Redd Foxx.

9. *Good Times* (1974–1979) was a spinoff of *Maude*, was developed and created by Norman Lear (Eric Monte and Mike Evans are also credited for the creation of the show). The storyline was relevant for the time (and still is) considering the despair and poor living conditions that so many Black families face in urban America. *Good Times* aired on CBS from 1974 to 1979.

10. *The Jeffersons* (1975–1985) was one of the longest running sitcoms on network TV (CBS). *The Jeffersons* was a spinoff of *All in the Family*. Many considered George Jefferson to be the complement to Archie Bunker. Both characters were bigoted and extremely opinionated. Notable fact: Roxie Roker, who played the role of Helen Willis, is the mother of rocker Lenny Kravitz. She passed away in 1995.

11. *Diff'rent Strokes* (1978–1986) made Gary Coleman a household name in America. The catchphrase "What you talkin bout Willis" became a popular saying by fans of the show during the late 1970s and early 1980s. Tragically, stars Gary Coleman, Dana Plato and Todd Bridges lives were plagued by legal woes and drug dependence. Of these three, Bridges is the only one still alive.

12. *The Cosby Show* (1984–1992), starring Bill Cosby, aired for eight seasons on NBC from 1984 until 1992. The show was groundbreaking because of its focus on an upper middle-class Black American family (the Huxtables) living in Brooklyn, New York. Cliff Huxtable (played by Bill Cosby) was a doctor; his wife Clair Huxtable (played by Phylicia Rashad) was a lawyer. The storylines and character roles depicted a strong Black nuclear family structure, which was a first for network TV.

13. *227* (1985–1990) aired on NBC from 1985 until 1990. The star of the show, Marla Gibbs, played the role of Mary Jenkins, a boisterous housewife who lives in the inner-city and is considered by her neighbors to be a gossipmonger. The series takes place in an apartment building numbered 227.

14. *Amen* (1986–1991): Deacon Frye, head of the First Community Church of Philadelphia, has a tendency to want to run everything. However the church hires a new assistant, Rev. Reuben Gregory, who has a different approach on how the church should function. After all, Rev. Reuben has been "called by God" to lead the flock. However, if Deacon Frye has his way, the good Reverend won't be leading the flock too far. The show stars actors Sherman Hemsley and Clifton Davis.

15. *A Different World* (1987–1993): The storyline for *A Different World* centers on a group of students who are attending a historically Black university and their struggle to make it through college. Lisa Bonet (Denise Huxtable from *The Cosby Show*), Kadeem Hardison and Jasmine Guy star in the show.

16. *Frank's Place* (1987–1988): Frank Parish (played by Tim Reid) is a college professor from Boston. He is notified that his father (who he has not seen in thirty-five years) has passed away and left him a restaurant in New Orleans. Frank has no interest in running a restaurant and wants to sell it to the employees, but is convinced otherwise. A curse is placed on him by Miss Marie (played by Frances E. Williams) which causes him to reconsider his intentions to sell. Scholars and critics have stated *Frank's Place* was a well written show that was short-changed in terms of its run on network television.

17. *Family Matters* (1989–1998) originated on ABC network from September 1989 to 1997 and then aired on CBS network from 1997 to 1998. A spin-off of *Perfect Strangers*, the series revolves around the

Winslow family, a middle-class African American family living in Chicago, Illinois. Midway through the first season, the show introduced the Winslows's nerdy neighbor Steve Urkel (played by Jaleel White), who quickly became its breakout character and eventually the show's main character.

18. *The Fresh Prince of Bel-Air* (1990–1996) starred Will Smith, who is considered one of the most sought after talents in Hollywood. The show was paramount considering its use of Hip Hop and Rap at times during the run of the series.

19. *In Living Color* (1990–1994) was an African American sketch comedy show which aired on the FOX network featuring the talents of the Wayans family. The show launched the careers of Keenen Ivory Wayans, Damon Wayans, David Allen Greer, Tommy Davidson and Jamie Foxx. Additionally, *In Living Color* was a jump start for the careers of Jennifer Lopez (one of the original Fly Girls) and comedic actor Jim Carrey.

20. *Martin* (1992–1997) played off the random misadventures of Martin Payne, an argumentative, brash, Detroit radio talk show host and his mixture of friends and foes.

21. *The Steve Harvey Show* (1996–2002) featured a former funk star named Steve Hightower (played by Steve Harvey) who enlisted as a high school music teacher away from his original career in Chicago. Writer/Producer Cedric the Entertainer plays the role of Cedric Jackie Robinson.

22. *The Bernie Mac Show* (2001–2006) (often shortened to *Bernie Mac* in syndication) is a sitcom that aired on FOX for five seasons from 2001 to 2006. The series featured comedic actor Bernie Mac and his wife Wanda raising his sister's three kids: Jordan, Vanessa, and Bryana.

23. *The Boondocks* (2005–) is the brainchild of cartoonist/creator Aaron McGruder. The storylines for *The Boondocks* frequently focus on socio-political commentary. The show bridges the gap and juxtaposes taboo subject matter around two central characters: Huey Freeman (who is ten and considered the voice of reason in the show although he reflects the mindset of Malcolm X and Huey Newton) and Riley Freeman who is eight, militant, and resistant to any type of paternal order.

24. *Tyler Perry's Meet the Browns* (2009–2012) created and produced by playwright, director, and producer Tyler Perry. *Tyler Perry's Meet the Browns* centers on a senior family living under one roof in Decatur, Georgia led by patriarch Mr. Brown and his daughter Cora Simmons. The show premiered in 2009 and finished its run in November, 2011 on TBS; it is an adaptation from Perry's play and film *Meet the Browns* (2004/2008). The show stars David Mann and Ta-

mela Mann, who starred in the earlier stage play and motion picture.

25. *The Cleveland Show* (2009–2013): No, this is not a show about Cleveland, Ohio (darn) but its focus is on a brother named Cleveland Brown (perhaps the creator Seth MacFarlane was thinking about the Cleveland Browns when he developed the show) who is the neighbor to deli owner Peter Griffin (*Family Guy*).

26. *black*-ish (2014–): A family man, Andre "Dre" Johnson struggles to gain a sense of cultural identity while raising his kids in a predominantly White, upper-middle-class neighborhood. "Dre considers himself the family patriarch and when he looks at his life—he sees a beautiful wife and four kids living happily in their colonial home in the 'burbs" (abc.go.com).

NOTES

1. Dr. Angela Nelson has published extensively in the subject area of Black popular culture and African Americans in television situation comedy. Other research interests include comic art, stage plays, the cultural significance of African American folk music, popular music, and religion. Dr. Nelson has edited *"This Is How We Flow": Rhythm in Black Cultures* (1999), and co-edited *Popular Culture Theory and Methodology: A Basic Introduction* (2006). She is an associate professor in the Department Of Popular Culture at Bowling Green State University.

2. Dr. Robin R. Means Coleman is the author of *Horror Noire: Blacks in American Horror Films from the 1890s to Present* (2011) and *African American Viewers and the Black Situation Comedy: Situating Racial Humor* (2000). Dr. Coleman is also the editor of *Say It Loud! African American Audiences, Media, and Identity* (2002) and co-editor of *Fight the Power! The Spike Lee Reader* (2008). She is a professor at the University of Michigan, Ann Arbor.

3. "A land flowing with milk and honey" is a reference to a biblical phrase that can be found in Exodus 33:3. "Go up to a land flowing with milk and honey; for I will not go up in your midst, because you are an obstinate people, and I might destroy you on the way." (NASB)

4. References/Sources: abc.go.com; imdb.com; famousfix.com.

Conclusion

What Am I?

From dust you have come, And to dust you shall return.
—Genesis 3:19 (The Voice)

What Am I?

A Forced Émigré
slave
victim
nigger.
One drop rule
Free Man
Segregation means . . .
separation.
Do you know
Jim Crow?
Back of the bus.
NAACP.
Rosa Parks.
Lynching, so many
hung on the tree . . .
For Whites Only.
KKK.
John Wayne.
For Colored Only.
Little Richard.
Pat Boone . . . Thief.
Elvis Presley . . . Thief.
Civil Rights.
Amos 'N' Andy.
Martin Luther King, Jr.
"I HAVE A DREAM!"
Malcolm X
"WE BEEN BAMBOOZLED!"
Integration, Cultural Assimilation,
White Neighborhoods.
Non-assimilation, Black Neighborhoods,
Ghettos.
Societal pressures Jews were restricted to-

Ghettos.
Economic pressures Niggers were restricted to-
Ghettos.
They say, "Try to mix."
Won't work.
They say "Vote."
The States say "Suppression."
They say "Vote."
We say Obama.
Hooray for Hollywood!
Halle Berry . . . Fine-looking, Halle Berry.
Natural beauty, natural hair, unblemished
skin that makes men stare.
Halle Berry, an American
Actress.
Monster's Ball,
Academy Award!
For doing the nasty with a White man . . . Miss Berry,
did he make you feel good?
In the end, Halle
you did win.
Hooray for Hollywood!
Denzel Washington, you are so talented,
you are so good.
An American Actor,
Training Day,
Academy Award!
You got cast to play a rogue cop in the hood.
Atlanta
"Chocolate City,"
Tyler Perry.
Madea's Family Reunion,
Tyler Perry.
Madea Goes to Jail,
Tyler Perry.
Madea's Big Happy Family.
MADEA, MADEA, MADEA!
TYLER PERRY, TYLER PERRY, TYLER PERRY!
Exploitation?
Yep.
Sell out?
Images of Coons and Buffoons?
Yep.
So What Am I?
Human being,
Spiritual being,
Emotional,
Psychological,
Husband,

Wife,
Daughter,
Son,
Sister,
Brother,
My Brotha,
My Sistah,
A soul created
and chosen by God . . .
Let the church say . . .
Amen.
Let the Church say . . .
Amen again.

AND ALL GOD'S CHILDREN SAID . . .

—David L. Moody

Appendix A

1. 1919, June 21. *Chicago Defender*, 9. ad—*Homesteader* (film); Oscar Micheaux; ad—Homesteader, an all-black cast film produced by Oscar Micheaux, is advertised.

2. 1920, January 31. *Chicago Defender*, 8. ad—*Within Our Gates* (film); Oscar Micheaux; ad—Within Our Gates, an all-black cast film produced by Oscar Micheaux is advertised.

3. 1928, May 19. "Stars That Shine." *Chicago Defender*. Billy Jones, 11. Spencer Williams; Spencer Williams, song writer, just returned from Europe after two years, where he wrote and directed several shows [and] has placed new songs with the Triangle Music Publishers in New York—"Talking About Home," "Shake It Down," and a great instrumental number, "Fireworks."

4. 1929, July 6. "Foster Plans Race Picture Company." *Afro-American* (Baltimore), 9. William Foster; Foster Photoplay Company; Pointing to the face that the race spends $8,000,000 a year to see the movies.

5. 1929, November 2. "Bill Foster Organizes Talkie Movie Company." *Chicago Defender*, 13. William Foster; Foster Photoplay Company; William Foster, veteran show promoted and writer of plays and the first man of his Race to introduce motion pictures in Chicago, his hometown, has organized the Foster Photo Play company in Los Angeles with its studios in this city.

6. 1929, December 21. "New Dunbar Theater." *Afro-American* (Baltimore), 8. ad—Scar of Shame (film); ad—Scar of Shame, an all-black motion picture, is advertised.

7. 1930, September 17. "Georgia Rose." *New York Amsterdam News*, 8. ad—Georgia Rose (film); Clarence Brooks; Evelyn Preer; Roberta Hyson; Spencer Williams.

8. 1939, September 30. "All-Colored Movie Field Has Weak Foundations; Producers Hit Each Other; Additional Ills Told." *New York*

Amsterdam News. Dan Burley, 16. William Foster; Oscar Micheaux; Eddie Green; Randol Rinaldo Productions; Once upon a time we took a stab at the status of the all-colored moving picture industry which is in what we chose to call its second infancy. At that time, we pointed out that subject matter and talent were two of the business' most glaring faults. Now we added a few more shortcomings plus some enlightening data that we didn't include in our first dissertation. Today, especially in New York, several productions are underway with a few hundred performers busy before the camera. Out in Hollywood, other pictures are in process of being filmed and on the surface, it looks like a prosperously fat season for Negro show business now creeping along on creaking legs.

9. 1947, March 20. Hollywood Spot – *Light Los Angeles Sentinel*. Earl Griffin, 21. *Body and Soul* (film); Canada Lee; Foxes of Harrow (film); Frank Yerby; Enterprise Studios' latest hit, "Body and Soul," now in the process of production, will prove to be the greatest film ever to leave Hollywood (from the [black viewer's] standpoint). . . . Frank Yerby's *Foxes of Harrow*, bought by Twentieth Century for a reputed $150,000, goes before the camera soon and will offer Sepia Hollywood more employment than they have enjoyed since *Stormy Weather*. I hear Suzette Johnson is being tested for the part of the high-spirited African princess.

10. 1950, March 11. "Is Paul Robeson Afraid?" *Afro-American* (Baltimore). Carl Murphy, 1. Paul Robeson; Discriminatory Practices; When Paul Robeson stepped off the train in Baltimore, recently, he was followed by an agent of the FBI. He is constantly under surveillance.

NOTE

1. Source: *Black Entertainers in African American Newspaper Articles: Vol. 1*; Charlene B. Regester.

Appendix B

Events from 1968 That Changed the Direction of How We View Racism in This Country

February 4	Rev. Dr. Martin Luther King, Jr. delivers a prophetic sermon at the Ebenezer Baptist Church in Atlanta. His sermon prophetically spoke to his service to God, mankind, and righteousness. Scholars have stated that on February 4, King preached his own eulogy.
March 16	Senator Robert Kennedy, former attorney general and brother of former president John F. Kennedy, announces that he will enter the 1968 presidential race (many felt Kennedy would be a composed, supportive voice in the White House for African Americans).
April 4	The Rev. Dr. Martin Luther King, Jr. spends the day working in Memphis with local leaders in preparation for the Poor People's March on Washington to take place in late April. At approximately 6 p.m. King is shot by James Earl Ray. Senator Robert Kennedy, who heard about the murder minutes before he was to give a speech in Indianapolis, IN, delivers a powerful impromptu eulogy in which he pleads with the audience for calm and peace. The King assassination sparks rioting in Baltimore, Boston, Chicago, Detroit, Kansas City, Newark, Washington, DC, and many other cities. Forty-six people were killed as a result of the riots.
June 4–5	On the night of the California primary Robert Kennedy addresses a large crowd of supporters at the Ambassador Hotel in San Francisco. He has won victories in California and South Dakota and is confident that his campaign will go on to unite the many factions stressing the country. As he leaves the stage at 12:13 a.m. on the morning of the fifth, Kennedy is shot by Sirhan Sirhan, a twenty-four-year-old Jordanian living in Los Angeles. The motive for the shooting is apparently anger at several pro-Israeli speeches Kennedy had made during the campaign. The forty-two-year-old Kennedy dies in the early morning of June sixth.
July 23	On July 23, 1968, in Cleveland's Glenville neighborhood, a confrontation took place between a number of African American men and police officers. Known as the "Glenville Shootout," the incident set off forty-eight hours of additional violence, as looting, arson fires, and beatings. Several people were killed and injured during the shootout. Residents blamed the lack of attention towards the needs of the Black community from the government (at the city, state, and federal level) with regard to economic

development, job creation, and unemployment as part of the problem (www.ohiohistorycentral.org/w/Glenville_Shootout).

August 8   The Republicans nominate Richard Nixon to be their presidential candidate. Nixon is challenged by fellow Republicans Nelson Rockefeller of New York and Ronald Reagan of California. Black Americans were skeptical about what Nixon's treatment toward the Black community would be. Their skepticism was warranted considering the disparaging remarks about Jews, Blacks, Italian-Americans, and Irish-Americans he made in a series of extended conversations with top aides and his personal secretary. His derogatory comments towards ethnic groups were recorded in the Oval Office sixteen months before he resigned as president.

September 1   Democratic nominee Hubert Humphrey kicks off his presidential campaign at New York City's Labor Day parade.

October 12   During the Summer Olympic Games in Mexico City, thirty-two African nations boycotted in protest of South Africa's participation. On October 18, Tommie Smith and John Carlos, athletes for the United States and medalists in the 200-meter dash, disrupted the games by performing the salutation towards Black Nationalism (Black power salute) during the "Star-Spangled Banner" at their medal ceremony. Smith and Carlos extended their Black gloved fists high to the sky in protest to the apartheid situation in South Africa.

November 5   Election Day. Nixon receives 43.4 percent of the total vote. Nixon is elected president.

December 11   The unemployment rate, at 3.3 percent, is the lowest it has been in fifteen years (as of January 2016 it is 4.9).

Data from cds.library.brown.edu/projects/1968/reference/timeline.html; www.bl s.gov/news.release/pdf/empsit.pdf.

Appendix C

John Amos (1939–)

A native of New Jersey, John Amos has a striking physique, and an outspoken and powerful image, which has made him one of the top actors in film and television. Amos was first employed as an advertising copywriter, social worker, and a semi-professional football player before starting his career in acting. He performed as a stand-up comic on the Greenwich Village circuit and his efforts ultimately led to his hiring as a staff writer on Leslie Ungums' musical variety show in 1969. Amos also starred on the *Mary Tyler Moore Show* (1970) as Gordy the weatherman. Additionally, he had recurring roles as the unemployed husband of maid Florida Evans (played by Esther Rolle) on the TV hit *Maude* (1972).

Amos has been critical of the industry's tactics of creating "so called" acting opportunities for Black actors that diminish their talents. Many of the character roles for actors in Hollywood can easily be labeled as stereotypes. Alternatively, Norman Lear's *Good Times* (1974) was meant to reverse that trend. *Good Times* is a situation comedy which was originally written to focus on urban Black family issues and the struggles of Black America, while also sharing family values; the setting is in a Chicago ghetto. However, Lear shifted the storyline to focus on the buffoonery of the Evan's teenage son J. J. (played by Jimmie Walker). Amos frequently spoke out against the script choices made by Lear which ultimately led to his removal from the show. In 1976, his character was killed in an off-camera car accident while finding employment out of state.

According to Amos:

> It ultimately reached a point where it was inflammable, I mean, spontaneous combustion could happen at any minute. They killed my character off and as God would have it, just when they told me I would never work again, I got cast in a little program called Roots, and as they would say, the rest is history. I could have begged and they made it obvious to me that if I wanted to come back and be a good boy . . . but I'd rather say "Toby be good nigger" in Roots than "Toby be good nigger" on *Good Times*. (Margretta Browne, blackfilm.com)

Amos was nominated for an Emmy for his role of the adult Kunte Kinte in the mini-series *Roots* (1977). Other film and TV credits include *Willa* (1979), *The Beastmaster* (1982), *Coming to America* (1988), *Love Boat, The A-Team, Murder She Wrote, One Life to Live, The West Wing,* and *The District.* He also appeared in the CBS series *Men in Trees.*

Eddie "Rochester" Anderson (1905–1977)

"Yes Sir Mr. Benny" was a familiar line delivered by Eddie "Roches-ter" Anderson on *The Jack Benny Program* (1950–1965). The son of a min-strel and circus tightrope walker, Eddie Anderson's gravel voice became his trademark to prominence. Anderson performed as one of the "Three Black Aces" with his brother, Cornelius, in 1924. In the early 1930s, he began to appear in films—he was featured in the role of "Noah" in *The Green Pastures* (1936). Other noteworthy film appearances include *Gone With The Wind* (1939), *Kiss the Boys Goodbye* (1941), *Cabin in the Sky* (1943), *It's a Mad, Mad, Mad, Mad World* (1963), and *Watermelon Man* (1970). In addition, Anderson was the first African American to have a recurring role on a national radio broadcast in the United States pairing with come-dian Jack Benny on his radio program in 1937. His rough voice, superb timing and comic relief to Benny's banter earned him a permanent spot as Benny's personal valet on the radio and TV programs (IMDb.com; "Eddie 'Rochester' Anderson." Bio. A&E Television Networks, 2015. Web. 02 May 2015).

Pearl Bailey (1918–1990)

Tony Award–winning singer and actress Pearl Bailey is known for her roles in works like *Carmen Jones, House of Flowers, Hello, Dolly!* and *Porgy and Bess.* Bailey also appeared many times on film and in television varie-ty programs, including *The Ed Sullivan Show* ("Pearl Bailey." Bio. A&E Television Networks, 2015. Web. 02 May 2015).

Harry Baird (1931–2005)

Harry Baird was a strong British actor who was cast in a number of racially motivated British films. His roles help to create a discourse re-garding the racial tensions in the United Kingdom during the 1950s and 1960s. Born in Guyana, he is best known to American audiences for his work as the Black American G.I. protagonist in Melvin Van Peebles's *Story of a Three-day Pass* (1968). Baird should also be remembered for his role as the victim of police cruelty in *Sapphire* (1959). He appeared in over thirty six movies and TV programs throughout his career.

James Baskett (1904–1948)

James Baskett is best known for his portrayal of Uncle Remus and singing the song "Zip-a-Dee-Doo-Dah" in the Disney feature film *Song of the South* (1946). His superb performance and portrayal of the famous Black storyteller earned him an Honorary Academy Award. Moreover, Baskett was the first Black male performer to receive an Oscar. Walt Disney's *Song of the South* is a feature length film which was produced and released by Disney in 1946. The storyline of the film focuses on Uncle Remus' "Tales of Brer Rabbit" that were articulated to a young boy named Johnny in an effort to help him cope with his concerns over his parents' separation as well as his new life on the plantation. The tales told by Uncle Remus are: "The Briar Patch," "The Tar Baby" and "Brer Rabbit's Laughing Place." However, according to Jim Korkis in his book *The Sad Song of the South*: "Song of the South came out in 1946 and there was no balance of media images. African American performers often portrayed comic roles where their characters were described as lazy, slow-witted, easily scared or flustered, subservient and worse. That image was what the American public was seeing and accepting as the norm for African Americans" (Korkis, 22). Controversial themes within the film regarding the racist character depiction of Uncle Remus continue to be a subject of debate.

Harry Belafonte (1927–)

Belafonte's career took off with the film *Carmen Jones* (1954). Musically, he had several hit songs—"The Banana Boat Song (Day-O)" and "Jamaica Farewell." In addition to his acting and singing career, Belafonte worked as an activist for several social and political causes. On the big screen, Belafonte and longtime friend Sidney Poitier collaborated on two successful film projects: *Buck and the Preacher* (1972) and *Uptown Saturday Night* (1974). Belafonte made numerous television appearances in the 70s and 80s, including a guest spot on *The Muppet Show* and a children's special *Free To Be . . . You and Me* (1974).

Belafonte starred with John Travolta in *White Man's Burden* (1995) and played the role of a callous gangster in Robert Altman's *Kansas City* (1996). He also appeared in *Bobby* (2006) a film about the assassination of Robert F. Kennedy ("Harry Belafonte." Bio. A&E Television Networks, 2015. Web. 02 May 2015).

Halle Berry (1966–)

Born on August 14, 1966, in Cleveland, Ohio, Halle Berry is an award-winning actress. She won an Academy Award for best actress for her performance in *Monster's Ball* (2001). She became the first African

American woman to win the honor. Currently, Berry is one of the highest-paid actresses in Hollywood.

Her breakthrough came when Spike Lee cast her as a crack addict in *Jungle Fever* (1991). In 1994, Berry gained a following from young movie goers for her performance as "Sharon Stone" in *The Flintstones* (1994). Berry joined the ranks of the "Bond Girls" as the character Jinx in the *James Bond* film *Die Another Day* (2002). Berry is also known for her role as "Storm" in *X2* (2003) the second installment of Marvel Comics's *X-Men*. Berry also starred in the film adaptation of DC Comics's *Catwoman* in which she played the lead character.

Other TV and film roles include *Introducing Dorothy Dandridge* (1999); *X-Men* (2000); *Gothika* (2003); *Their Eyes Were Watching God* (2005); voiceover talent for *Robots*; *X-Men: The Last Stand* (2006); *Perfect Stranger*, costarring Bruce Willis (2007); *The Call* (2013); *X-Men: Days of Future Past* (2014); and the CBS sci-fi series *Extant* (2014–2015) produced by Steven Spielberg ("Halle Berry." Bio. A&E Television Networks, 2015. Web. 26 April 2015).

Diahann Carroll (1935–)

Diahann Carroll is an actress of stage, screen, and TV known for her show *Julia* (1968) and films such as *I Know Why the Caged Bird Sings* (1979). Carroll was also nominated for an Academy Award for *Claudine* in 1974. Her "white collar" nurse role in *Julia* made her the first African American woman to star in her own network prime-time television program. She was nominated for an Emmy for *Julia* in 1969 and won the Golden Globe Award in 1968 ("Diahann Carroll." Bio. A&E Television Networks, 2015. Web. 02 May 2015).

Dave Chappelle (1973–)

Dave Chappelle is a comedian whose Comedy Central show, *Chappelle's Show*, became a hit in 2003. He received two Emmy Award nominations for the popular show, which frequently addressed controversial issues regarding race relations in the United States. In 2006, he unexpectedly quit the show and moved to a farm in Ohio.

Chappelle began making appearances in films such as *Robin Hood: Men In Tights* (1993) and *Half Baked* (1994). Chappelle starred in *The Nutty Professor* (1996) alongside Eddie Murphy; *Killin' Them Softly* in (2000); and *Undercover Brother* in (2002). Currently, Chappelle is back on stage doing a one man show on tour.

Bill Cosby (1937–)

Bill Cosby is one of the world's most well-known entertainers and comedians. In his early twenties, he appeared on many variety programs including *The Ed Sullivan Show* and *the Johnny Carson Show*. His big break came in 1965 when he was cast as "Alexander Scott" in *I Spy* (1965). Cosby created *Filmation*, a cartoon based on many of his high school buddies including "Weird Harold," "Dumb Donald," "Mushmouth," and others. The program became known as *Fat Albert and the Cosby Kids* (1972). The theme from *Fat Albert and the Cosby Kids* was based on Cosby's dissertation for his doctorate in Education from the University of Massachusetts. Cosby's film credits include *Uptown Saturday Night* (1974), *Let's Do It Again* (1975), *A Piece of the Action* (1977), *Mother, Jugs & Speed* (1976), *California Suite* (1978) and *The Devil and Max Devlin* (1981). Cosby was also one of the original cast members of *The Electric Company* (1971), and he was featured in the series *Pinwheel* (1979).

In 1984 the hit TV program *The Cosby Show* began production with a storyline portraying a White-collar family with a father employed as a physician and the mother as a lawyer. Originally rejected by ABC, NBC picked it up and the show became a hit on network television during the 1980s. Furthermore, the program broke Nielsen viewing records with Cosby becoming known as "America's Favorite Dad." Perhaps the strongest messages delivered from the show were the positive images of a professional Black family and a united Black family structure. *The Cosby Show* will go down in history as one of the most popular shows to air on network television and off-network syndication. What's more, *The Cosby Show* was a strong anchor and lead-in for the NBC Thursday night line-up which included, *Night Court* (1984), *Hill Street Blues* (1981), and *Family Ties* (1982).

In spite of the success, Cosby had concerns regarding how minorities were portrayed on television. In 1987 he produced the TV series *A Different World* and insisted that it should follow *The Cosby Show* rather than *Family Ties*. The setting for *A Different World* was at a historically Black college and the storyline focused on adolescence and education.

The Cosby Show finally ended in 1992 with the final production considered to be one of the highest-rated shows of the season.

Dorothy Dandridge (1922–1964)

Born on November 9, 1922, in Cleveland, Ohio, Dorothy Dandridge sang at Harlem's Cotton Club and Apollo Theatre and became the first African American woman to be nominated for an Academy Award for best actress. Her lead role in *Carmen Jones* (1954), a film adaptation of Bizet's opera *Carmen* that also co-starred Harry Belafonte, pushed her to fame and fortune. With her eye-catching looks and charismatic style,

Dandridge became the first African American to earn an Academy Award nomination for best actress ("Dorothy Dandridge." Bio. A&E Television Networks, 2015. Web. 02 May 2015).

Sammy Davis Jr. (1925–1990)

Davis's films include *Porgy and Bess* (1959), *Ocean's 11* (1960), *Robin and the Seven Hoods* (1964) (with fellow Rat Pack members Frank Sinatra and Dean Martin), *Sweet Charity* (1968) *That's Dancing!* (1985) and *Tap* (1989). Davis's greatest success as a performer was during the 1950s and 1960s; he continued to entertain and record until the late 1980s. Davis is best known for his work as part of the "Rat Pack," with Frank Sinatra, Dean Martin, Peter Lawford, and Joey Bishop ("Sammy Davis Jr." Bio. A&E Television Networks, 2015. Web. 01 April 2015).

Ossie Davis (1917–2005)

Akin to Sidney Poitier, throughout his career Ossie Davis spoke out against the stereotypical roles that were frequently offered to Black American actors. Davis often brought self-respect to the characters he played, including those with lowly jobs or from underprivileged backgrounds.

His early acting jobs on Broadway paved the way for a long career in television and film. Davis starred in several films including *The Cardinal* (1963), *School Daze* (1988), *Do the Right Thing* (1989), *Doctor Dolittle* (1998), and *Jungle Fever* (2001); his career spanned five decades.

He also appeared on television in the mini-series *Roots: The Next Generation* (1979), *Evening Shade* (1990–1994), *Touched by an Angel* (1996–2002), and *The L Word* (2004–2005).

In addition to acting, Davis is known as a trailblazer for his early efforts as an African American director and producer. His most notable directing credit is *Cotton Comes to Harlem* (1970) ("Ossie Davis." Bio. A&E Television Networks, 2015. Web. 03 May 2015).

Ruby Dee (1922–2014)

Ruby Dee is best known for starring in the film adaptation *A Raisin in the Sun* (1961). The film was based off the play by Lorraine Hansberry that debuted on Broadway in 1959. Dee played alongside Sidney Poitier in the film. Other TV and film credits include *Roots: The Next Generation* (1979), the PBS special *Zora Is My Name*, and *Do the Right Thing (1989)*. In 1991, Dee won an Emmy Award for her work on the television movie *Decoration Day*.

Taye Diggs (1972–)

Taye Diggs is an actor known for his role in the musical "Rent" and in films such as *How Stella Got Her Groove Back* (1998); *The Best Man* (1999); *Go* (1999); and *The Best Man Holiday* (2013). Television credits include *Ally McBeal* (2001), *The West Wing* (2003), *Kevin Hill* (2004–2005), *Will & Grace* (2006), *Day Break* (2006–2007), *Private Practice* (2007–2013), *Grey's Anatomy* (2007–2013) and *The Good Wife* (2014) ("Taye Diggs." Bio. A&E Television Networks, 2015. Web. 03 May 2015).

Redd Foxx (1922–1991)

John Elroy Sanford better known as "Redd Foxx" was an African American comedian and actor. Like so many other Black performers, Foxx left home at an early age and performed on the "Chitlin Circuit" during the 1940s and 1950s. The "Chitlin Circuit" was a name given to several venues (Black nightclubs, juke joints, theaters) throughout the eastern, southern, and mid-west areas of the United States where Black actors, comedians, and musicians could perform. These venues targeted Black audiences and were considered safe environments for Black entertainment during the period of Jim Crow and racial segregation. Although his stand-up comedy routines were considered vulgar and racy (especially for White audiences) critics have stated that Foxx paved the way for many comics; especially names such as George Carlin and Lenny Bruce.

Foxx is best known for his successful run of the TV situation comedy *Sanford and Son* which aired on NBC from 1972 to 1977. After leaving television he continued with his stand-up comedy work in Las Vegas. Additionally, Foxx is also known for his role as Bennie Wilson in the film *Harlem Nights* (1989) with Eddie Murphy ("Redd Foxx." Bio. A&E Television Networks, 2015. Web. 19 June 2015).

Lena Horne (1917–2010)

Actress and singer Lena Horne was known for films such as *The Wiz* and her trademark song, "Stormy Weather." Horne was the first Black performer to be signed to a long-term contract by a major Hollywood studio (*NY Times*). Similar to Sidney Poitier, Ossie Davis, and Ruby Dee, Horne refused to accept roles that stereotyped African Americans. However, her resistance to be cast in certain roles became a topic of controversy for many Black actors in Hollywood who would take the stereotypical roles ("Lena Horne." Bio. A&E Television Networks, 2015. Web. 03 May 2015; topics.nytimes.com/).

Rex Ingram (1895–1969)

Rex (Clifford) Ingram graduated from Northwestern University with a degree in medicine before launching a brilliant acting career which spanned fifty years. Ingram made his screen debut during the silent era in *Tarzan of the Apes* (1918). He received widespread acclaim for his portrayal of "De Lawd" in *The Green Pastures* (1936). Ingram also appeared on the Broadway stage and in television productions. Ingram is probably best remembered for his portrayal of Jim, the fugitive slave, opposite Mickey Rooney in *The Adventures of Huckleberry Finn* (1939). Additionally, Ingram appeared in several television programs such as *I Spy* (1965), *Daktari* (1967–1968), *Gunsmoke* (1969), and *The Bill Cosby Show* (1969).

Samuel L. Jackson (1948–)

Samuel L. Jackson is considered one of the highest paid actors of all time and is best known for work with filmmaker Spike Lee. Notable films include *Pulp Fiction* (1994); *Do The Right Thing* (1989); *Coming to America* (1988); *Mo' Better Blues* (1990); *Jungle Fever* (1991); *Goodfellas* (1990). Most recent hits include *The Avengers* (2012); *Django Unchained* (2012); *Captain America: The Winter Soldier* (2014); *Avengers: Age of Ultron* (2015). Jackson is also a Spoke-Celebrity for Capital One.

Duane Jones (1937–1988)

Duane Jones was born on February 2, 1936 in New York City, New York. His academic and theatrical accomplishments included serving as the head of the Literature Department at Antioch College (1972–1976). He also taught literature at Long Island University, was the director of the Maguire Theater at the State University College at Old Westbury and artistic director at the Richard Allen Center for Culture and Art in Manhattan. Jones was also executive director of the Black Theater Alliance, a federation of theater companies, from 1976 to 1981. His acting stage credits include the Negro Ensemble Company, the Actors Playhouse, and the National Black Theater. In addition to *Night of the Living Dead*, Jones is known for his acting work in television and roles in such films as *Ganja and Hess*, *Beat Street*, and *Losing Ground* (C. Gerald Fraserny, NY Times.com). Jones is best known for his role as Ben in the cult horror thriller *Night of the Living Dead* (1968). The controversial casting of Duane Jones paved the way for the casting of African Americans in lead roles.

James Earl Jones (1931–)

James Earl Jones was the voice of "Darth Vader" in *Star Wars* (1977), *The Empire Strikes Back* (1980), and *Return of the Jedi* (1983). He's also known for roles in such films as *The Hunt for Red October* and *Field of*

Dreams. Because of the unique quality of his deep voice, Jones was often cast in character roles that displayed strong and authoritative traits. He played a Navy admiral in *The Hunt for Red October* (1990), *Patriot Games* (1992) and *Clear and Present Danger* (1994). Jones was also voice-over talent for the animated film *The Lion King*. Jones won a pair of Emmy Awards in 1991, for his leading role on the dramatic series *Gabriel's Fire* (1990–91) and his supporting role on the miniseries *Heat Wave* ("James Earl Jones." Bio. A&E Television Networks, 2015. Web. 03 May 2015).

Quincy Jones (1933–)

Quincy Jones began composing for film and television in the mid-sixties and eventually produced over fifty scores. He has worked with musicians Michael Jackson, Frank Sinatra, Aretha Franklin and Celine Dion. Jones founded Qwest Productions, for which he arranged and produced hugely successful albums by Frank Sinatra and other major pop figures. In 1978, he produced the soundtrack for the musical adaptation of *The Wizard of Oz*, *The Wiz*, starring Michael Jackson and Diana Ross. In 1982, Quincy Jones produced Michael Jackson's all-time best-selling album *Thriller* ("Quincy Jones." Bio. A&E Television Networks, 2015. Web. 12 March 2015).

Arsenio Hall (1956–)

Cleveland native Arsenio Hall is an actor, comedian and is recognized for being the first Black late-night talk show host for his groundbreaking show, *The Arsenio Hall Show* which aired on FOX from 1989 to 1994. Notable film appearances include *Amazon Women on the Moon* (1987), *Coming to America* (1988), and *Harlem Nights* (1989). In 2013 FOX hired Hall again to host a late-night talk show. Hall used the show as a showcase for rap and hip-hop artists. The show was cancelled in 2014.

Hall attended Ohio University in Athens, Ohio, and majored in communications. He transferred and graduated from Kent State University in Kent, Ohio. Like many Black actors, Hall started out in advertising and switched to stand-up comedy. Singer Nancy Wilson discovered Hall performing at a comedy club which ultimately created an opportunity for Hall to open for musicians such as Aretha Franklin, Tom Jones, Patti Labelle, Wayne Newton, and Tina Turner.

Hall appeared on various comedy and musical shows including, *Solid Gold*, *Motown Revue* and *The New Love American Style*; he also hosted a show called *The Half-Hour Comedy Hour*. Hall made his feature film debut in *Amazon Women on the Moon* in 1987 ("Arsenio Hall." Bio. A&E Television Networks, 2015. Web. 22 March 2015).

Catherine L. Hughes (1947–)

Radio One, Inc. is led by Chairperson and Founder, Catherine L. Hughes. She has over 40 plus years of operating experience in radio/TV broadcasting. Cathy Hughes owns and operates over fifty radio stations; her company also owns and operates TV One (www.tvone.tv). TV One is a 24–hour entertainment network designed to entertain, inform, and to promote Black popular culture. Launched in January 2004, TV One is available in over fifty-seven million homes. Hughes has become one of the most powerful and influential Black American woman in broadcasting and Cable (www.radio-one.com/our-properties/tv-one/).

Woodie King Jr. (1937–)

Woodie King Jr. was born on July 27, 1937 in Mobile, Alabama, USA. He is an actor and director, known for *Men in Black 3* (2012), *Serpico* (1973) and *Death of a Prophet* (1981).

Eartha Kitt (1928–2008)

On the big screen, Kitt starred opposite Nat "King" Cole in the W. C. Handy biography *St. Louis Blues* (1958). In 1959, she starred opposite Sammy Davis Jr. and received an Academy Award nomination for her role as the character *Anna Lucasta* (1959). In the late 1960s, Kitt played one of her most famous roles—the evil "Catwoman" on the television series *Batman* starring Adam West and Burt Ward (1966–1968). Kitt's claim to fame on the show was her distinguishing voice, sensuous moves, and signature "purrrr-fect" line; all of which made her a hit. Kitt also received a Daytime Emmy Award for her vocal performance on the animated children's series *The Emperor's New School*.

Spike Lee (1957–)

Producer, director, writer and actor Spike Lee creates films that explore race matters and raise questions regarding the political climate in the United States. Notable films include *She's Gotta Have It* (1986), *Do the Right Thing* (1989), *Malcolm X* (1992), and *Bamboozled* (2000). Lee's film, *Do The Right Thing*, was nominated for an Academy Award for Best Original Screenplay in 1989. The film focused on race relations, urban violence, and political concerns in America. Succeeding films, such as *Malcolm X*, *Mo' Better Blues* (1990), *Summer of Sam* (1999) and *She Hate Me* (2004) also addressed social and civil rights concerns. Lee's film *4 Little Girls*, a piece about the 1963 16th Street Baptist Church bombing, was nominated for an Academy Award for Best Feature Documentary in 1997.

In 2006, Lee directed and produced a four-hour documentary for television, *When the Levees Broke: A Requiem in Four Acts*, about life in New Orleans in the aftermath of Hurricane Katrina.

Lee has also had commercial success in directing television commercials. Most notable TV spots are for Nike, Converse, Taco Bell and Ben & Jerry's. His production company, 40 Acres & A Mule Filmworks, is located in his old stomping grounds (where he grew up) of Fort Green in Brooklyn ("Spike Lee." Bio. A&E Television Networks, 2015. Web. 19 February 2015).

Hattie McDaniel (1895–1952)

Before Halle there was Hattie! Film actress and radio performer Hattie McDaniel became the first African American to win an Oscar in 1940, for her supporting role as Mammy in *Gone with the Wind*. McDaniel performed on radio and TV for many years ("Hattie McDaniel." Bio. A&E Television Networks, 2015. Web. 02 May 2015).

Nina Mae McKinney (1913–1967)

Nina Mae McKinney is known as the seductress "Chick" from *Hallelujah* (1929), the first all-Black, all-sound musical. Even though she was acknowledged as a great actress, singer and dancer by audiences in the United States and Europe, today, very little is mentioned about her career (IMDb).

Claudia McNeil (1917–1993)

Claudia McNeil acted in many films including *The Last Angry Man* (1959). She also appeared in the TV series *The DuPont Show of the Month* (1957), *The Nurses* (1962), *Roll of Thunder, Hear My Cry* (1978), and *Roots: The Next Generations* (1979) (*Black Women in America An Historical Encyclopedia* Volumes 1 and 2, edited by Darlene Clark Hine Carlson Publishing Inc., Brooklyn, New York www.aaregistry.org/).

Oscar Micheaux (1884–1951)

Before Spike there was Oscar! While mainstream Hollywood filmmakers demeaned the images of Black Americans on the silver screen, an underground movement gave rise to a group of independent Black filmmakers who flourished during the late 1920s and 1930s (Bogle, 102). Early Black filmmakers such as Oscar Micheaux (who is credited as the first African American to produce and direct a feature film), tried to present positive images and realistic portrayals of Black America. However, he was frequently afflicted by financial concerns, technical issues, problems with distribution, and controversial storylines. Oscar Micheaux's 1920 film, *Within Our Gates*, sparked a controversy because of an explosive lynching sequence. The fear that it might inspire race riots caused the Chicago Board of Censors to originally reject the film. When the film finally opened in Chicago its national distribution was limited. Southern theaters refused to book it; it later disappeared (Bogle, 116). Micheaux was at the center of controversy again in 1938 when the Young Communist League boycotted his film *God's Stepchildren* (1938). The boycott, which involved picketing the RKO Theatre at the Harlem premiere, declared that the film "creates a false splitting of Negroes in to light and Dark groups" (Gaines, 126). The splitting of the races was a discriminatory practice used by White employers in Harlem. Employers would often divide workers against each other based on skin color. However, it is worth noting that the boycott was organized as a recruiting tool for Black membership by the Young Communist League. On one hand, Micheaux has been criticized for selecting actors with a light pigment for prominent roles, for selecting genres of film that imitate Hollywood, and for his poor standards in technical quality. On the other hand, Donald Bogle points out that films such as *God's Step Children*, reflects the racial philosophy of the Black middle classes in the 1930s and 1940s (115). Micheaux, a voice for Black Americans from 1919 to 1950, will be remembered as one of the most prolific Black filmmakers in American cinema history.

Mantan Moreland (1902–1973)

Born in Monroe, Louisiana in 1902, his acting career began early. Moreland, reportedly, ran away from home several times to join the circus. It was during his many run away attempts to the circus that he began to develop and sharpen his comedic skills. By the late 1920s, Moreland began making the rounds through "The Chitlin' Circuit," performing on Broadway and touring Europe. At the outset, Moreland appeared in low-budget "race movies" aimed at African American audiences, but as his comedic talents came to be recognized, he received roles in larger productions and his career began to flourish during 1940s and 50s. He was well known for his role as Birmingham Brown in the Charlie Chan Movies (*The Jade Mask, The Chinese Ring, The Feathered Serpent, The Golden Eye*—1945–1948). However, it was his role as Jeff in *King of the Zombies* (a cult classic) that became his signature film.

Problematic for many was the fact that Moreland was often cast in roles as a buffoon. Over and over again he was referred to as the man with the fastest eyes in the West (Bogle, 72). According to Donald Bogle, "sometimes Moreland's small stature elevated him from mere coon to a symbol of the universal little man" (74). In 1957 Moreland appeared in an off-Broadway, all-Black production of *Waiting for Godot*. Additionally, he had minor roles in *The Comic* (1969) and *Watermelon Man* (1970).

Etta Moten (1901–2004)

In addition to her vocal dubbing and on-screen film credits, Etta Moten played the role of Bess in the 1943 revival of *Porgy and Bess*. Also a radio journalist, Etta interviewed Dr. Martin Luther King Jr. after the ceremonies in Ghana on March 6, 1957, and conducted her own radio show for WMAQ/NBC in Chicago for many years. Etta Moten became the first African American stage and screen star to sing and perform at the White House (at the invitation of President and Mrs. Franklin D. Roosevelt) on January 31, 1933 (*African American Registry*, www. aaregistry.org).

Eddie Murphy (1961–)

At a young age, stand-up comedian Eddie Murphy joined the cast of NBC's *Saturday Night Live*. Additionally, Murphy co-starred with Nick Nolte in *48 Hours* (1982) and went on to further box-office success in *Trading Places* (1983), *Beverly Hills Cop* (1984), *Coming to America* (1988), *The Nutty Professor* (1996), *Doctor Dolittle* (1998) and *Norbit* (2007).

Maidie Norman (1912–1998)

Maidie Norman began her career in radio with appearances on *The Jack Benny Program* and *Amos 'n' Andy*. Norman made her film debut in the 1947 film *The Peanut Man*. Norman later appeared in supporting roles in *Torch Song* (1953), *Bright Road* (1953), *Susan Slept Here* (1954), *The Opposite Sex* (1956), and *Written on the Wind* (1956). In the 1970s and 1980s, she guest starred on episodes of *Good Times*, *The Jeffersons*, *Little House on the Prairie* and *The Streets of San Francisco*. Her last film role was in *Terrorist on Trial: The United States vs. Salim Ajami* (1988) and that same year she made her last three television appearances in *Amen*, the television film *Side by Side*, and an episode of *Simon & Simon*. One of her most memorable roles was as the ill-fated housekeeper Elvira Stitt in Robert Aldrich's 1962 horror film *What Ever Happened to Baby Jane?*—playing opposite Bette Davis and Joan Crawford (Bob McCann, *Encyclopedia of African American Actresses in Film and Television* [Jefferson: McFarland and Company, Inc., 2010], 253–254).

Lupita Nyong'o (1983–)

Lupita Amondi Nyong'o was born March 1, 1983 in Mexico City, Mexico, to Kenyan parents Dorothy and Peter Anyang' Nyong'o. She is a graduate from the Yale School of Drama's acting program. She won an Academy Award for Best Supporting Actress in 2014 for her role as Patsey in *12 Years a Slave* (2013). She was also the lead in MTV's award-winning drama series, *Shuga* (2009), appeared in the thriller *Non-Stop*

(2014), and will have roles in the film's *Star Wars: Episode VII — The Force Awakens* (2015) and *The Jungle Book* (2016).

Her stage credits include playing *Perdita* in *The Winter's Tale*, (Yale Repertory Theater), Sonya in *Uncle Vanya*, Katherine in *The Taming of the Shrew*, as well as being in the original production of Michael Mitnick's "*Elijah*."

Hubert B. Payne (1938–2006)

Hubert B. Payne, is the former station owner of WOIO-TV *Channel Nineteen*. Additionally, Payne was the first African American local sales manager at a network owned and operated television station (WKYC-TV/Cleveland) in the United States. Payne won a construction permit for a new channel (19) in the early 80s becoming one of the early Black pioneers to build a major market television station from the ground up (the first Black owned TV station was WGPR-TV in Detroit. It went on the air in 1975; the station was owned by William V. Banks). Payne signed WOIO-TV on the air on May 19, 1985. He sold the station to Malrite Communications Group, Inc. in 1986.

Melvin Van Peebles (1932–)

Melvin Van Peebles (he is also the father of Mario Van Peebles) is an actor, director, screenwriter, playwright, novelist and composer. He is most famous for creating the acclaimed film *Sweet Sweetback's Baadasssss Song* (1971), which signaled a new era and genre of African American theme based films (*Blaxploitation*).

Tyler Perry (1969–)

Writer, actor, producer, and director Tyler Perry has built an entertainment empire that consists of successful films, plays, and publications. Television credits include *If Loving You Is Wrong* (2014–2015); *For Better or Worse* (2013–2014); *The Haves and the Have Nots*; *House of Payne*; *Meet The Browns* (2009). Perry's film credits include *Teenage Mutant Ninja Turtles 2* (2016); *Tyler Perry's Madea's Tough Love* (2015); *Tyler Perry's A Madea Christmas* (2013); *For Colored Girls* (2010); *Madea Goes to Jail* (2009); *Madea's Family Reunion* (2006). Perry's state of the art studios in Atlanta, Georgia are considered one of the best production facilities in the world.

Sidney Poitier (1927–)

Sidney Poitier became the first Black Academy Award winner for Best Actor in 1964, receiving the honor for his performance in *Lilies of the Field* (1963). Cast mainly in supporting roles, Poitier had a career breakthrough with *Blackboard Jungle* (1955). He scored his first Academy Award nomination for the 1958 crime drama *The Defiant Ones* with Tony Curtis. The following year, Poitier was a huge success as a leading man in the musical *Porgy and Bess*, co-starring with Dorothy Dandridge. This film and his impressive performance in 1961's *A Raisin in the Sun* helped make him a top box office star.

In 1964, Poitier won an Academy Award for best actor for his performance in *Lilies of the Field* (1963)—marking the first Oscar win by an African American actor. In 1967, he had two very strong performances as the Philadelphia detective Virgil Tibbs in the Southern crime drama *In the Heat of the Night*, and in *Guess Who's Coming to Dinner*. Poitier broke barriers playing the role of Dr. John Prentice, a Black man engaged to a White woman in *Guess Who's Coming to Dinner* (1967). The film forced America to take a closer look at interracial marriage and the anti-miscegenation laws in the United States. Miscegenation laws were ruled as unconstitutional in 1967 by the U.S. Supreme Court in the *Loving v. Virginia* case. Katharine Hepburn and Spencer Tracy played the fiancée's parents in the film ("Sidney Poitier." Bio. A&E Television Networks, 2015. Web. 09 May 2015).

Oscar Polk (1899–1949)

Polk was an actor, known for *Gone with the Wind* (1939), *The Green Pastures* (1936) and *Cabin in the Sky* (1943).

Evelyn Preer (1896–1932)

Evelyn Preer, one of the first African American silent screen actresses to transition into sound Hollywood films, was born on July 21, 1896 in Vicksburg, Mississippi. After her father's death, Preer and her mother relocated to Chicago, Illinois where she completed high school before pursuing acting. Preer's big break came when she landed a role in Oscar Micheaux's first film, *The Homesteader* (1919), in which she played a tragically unhappy woman abandoned by her husband for a mulatto woman whom he believed to be White. Impressed by her talent, Micheaux cast Preer in several roles in which she generally played dramatic characters, challenging many of the prevailing black film stereotypes. Preer expanded her acting abilities into the area of theater, frequently alternating between the screen and stage as she became a staple for Micheaux's dramatic films and an esteemed actress for the Lafayette Players ("Evelyn Preer" blackpast.org. 2015. Web. 03 May. Contributor, Adrienne Warttts).

Other films include *The Brute* (1920), *The Gunsaulus Mystery* (1921), *Deceit* (1923), *Birthright* (1924), *The Devil's Disciple* (1925), *The Conjure Woman* (1926), and *The Spider's Web* (1926) (www.aaregistry.org).

Richard Pryor (1940–2005)

Richard Pryor was a comedian, actor, film director, social critic, satirist, writer, and MC. Pryor was known for his extreme analyses of discrimination and current event issues. His expressive viewpoints were often framed through the use of profanity, as well as racial monikers. However, his creative storytelling style and quick wit propelled him into "Rock Star" status. Pryor is regarded as one of the most important and influential stand-up comedians of all time.

Pryor's work includes concert movies and recordings: Richard Pryor: *Live & Smokin'* (1971), *That Nigger's Crazy* (1974) . . . *Is It Something I Said?* (1975), *Bicentennial Nigger* (1976), *Richard Pryor: Live in Concert* (1979), *Richard Pryor: Live on the Sunset Strip* (1982), and *Richard Pryor: Here and Now* (1983). He also starred in several films as an actor, such as *Superman III* (1983), but was usually in comedies such as *Silver Streak* (1976), and occasionally in dramatic roles, such as Paul Schrader's film *Blue Collar* (1978). He teamed up on many projects with actors/writers Gene Wilder and Paul Mooney.

Shonda Rhimes (1970–)

Shonda Rhimes is best known for her work as the creator, head writer, executive producer and showrunner of the medical drama television series *Grey's Anatomy*, *Private Practice*, *Scandal*, and *How to Get Away with Murder*. In May 2007, Rhimes was named one of TIME magazine's 100 people who help shape the world. Rhimes attended Dartmouth College, where she majored in English and film studies and earned her Bachelor's degree in 1991. She was awarded an honorary doctorate from Dartmouth 2014. She also has a Master of Fine Arts (MFA) from the University of Southern California's School of Cinema-Television.

The World of "ShondaLand": *Grey's Anatomy* (2005–present), *Private Practice* (2007–2013), *Scandal* (2012–present), and *How to Get Away with Murder* (2014–present).

Bill "Bojangles" Robinson (1878–1949)

Bill "Bojangles" Robinson was a Black American tap dancer and actor best known for his stage performances on Broadway and film roles. In 1928, he starred on Broadway in the hugely successful musical revue *Blackbirds of 1928*, which featured his famous "stair dance." *Blackbirds* was a revue starring African American performers, intended for White audiences.

Robinson starred in several Hollywood films opposite child star Shirley Temple. His film credits include *Rebecca of Sunnybrook Farm*, *The Little Colonel*, and *Stormy Weather*, co-starring Lena Horne and Cab Calloway.

Robinson celebrated his sixty first birthday in public by dancing sixty one blocks of Broadway ("Bill "Bojangles" Robinson." Bio. A&E Television Networks, 2015. Web. 02 May 2015).

Max Robinson (1939–1988)

A graduate of Oberlin College, Max Robinson was a broadcast journalist for several stations during his career. Robinson's career began in radio at WSSV-AM (Petersburg, VA) and WANT-AM (Richmond, VA). His television career started at WTOV in Portsmouth, VA. While working at WTOV Robinson's station management would not permit him to deliver the news in front of the camera. The viewers could hear his voice behind the station logo, but they could not see his face. Robinson decided to share with the viewers "the man behind the logo" one day. Because of his decision to be seen on camera, he was fired by the station.

From WTOV-TV he moved to Washington, DC working to become the first African American anchor for WRC-TV. He also worked for WTOP-TV (now WUSA-TV) in Washington, DC. Robinson won two Emmy Awards for his documentary *The Other Washington*. The documentary depicted the life of Black Americans in the District of Columbia.

Most notably, Robinson is known for being the first African American broadcast network news anchor serving as co-anchor for ABC *World News Tonight*. In 1978, ABC *News* revamped their nightly news broadcast into *World News Tonight*. Roone Arledge hired Robinson to become part of a new three-anchor format that included Peter Jennings in London and Frank Reynolds as the lead anchor in Washington. Robinson would anchor national news from Chicago.

Controversy surrounded much of Robinson's career with ABC *News*. He frequently had disagreements with management over the negative portrayal of Black America in their newscasts. Robinson's tenure with ABC *News* ended in 1984 when he left to become the first African American anchor at WMAQ-TV in Chicago. Additionally, Robinson is one of the founding members of NABJ (National Association of Black Journalists).

Esther Rolle (1920–1998)

A stage, film and TV actress, Esther Rolle is best remembered as Florida Evans—a character she played on two comedy series, *Maude* and *Good Times*. Audiences adored her character so much that Lear created *Good Times* especially for her.

Good Times premiered in February 1974, and soon became a hit. In the series, Florida Evans lived with her family in one of Chicago's high-rise housing projects. John Amos played her husband, and both Amos and Rolle wanted the show to present strong positive role models for the

African American community. While the show had some promising moments in its early days, some felt that it perpetuated stereotypes about urban Blacks. The show often focused on the buffoonery of the eldest son J. J., played by Jimmie Walker, who created the national catchphrase "Dyn-o-mite." Both Amos and Role left the show in frustration (Amos left in 1976 and Rolle left in 1977). However, Norman Lear talked Rolle into coming back for the 1978–1979 season by promising content changes. The show was canceled in 1979.

Rolle won the Outstanding Supporting Actress in a Limited Series or a Special Emmy Award in 1979 for *Summer of My German Soldier*. Rolle also found roles in such films as *Driving Miss Daisy* (1990), *How to Make an American Quilt* (1995) and *Down in the Delta* (1998), which was directed by poet Maya Angelou ("Esther Rolle." Bio. A&E Television Networks, 2015. Web. 02 May 2015).

Cicely Tyson (1924–)

Tyson has won accolades and awards for her performances on TV, the stage, and in film, with credits including *Sounder, Roots, The Autobiography of Miss Jane Pittman*, and *The Help*. Tyson has won two Emmy Awards and a Tony Award, among other honors, over the course of her acting career. She was inducted into the Black Filmmakers Hall of Fame. Tyson was nominated for an Academy Award for 1972's *Sounder*. She also portrayed notable roles on television, including Kunta Kinte's mother in the adaptation of Alex Haley's *Roots* and the title role in The Autobiography of Miss Jane Pittman, which earned Tyson an Emmy Award in 1974.

However, Tyson's career path was not a smooth one. Tyson was selective about the roles she did; she refused to do "Blaxploitation" films which limited her opportunities for work during the 1970s.

Tyson recently appeared in *The Help* (2011), several Tyler Perry movies, and *How to Get Away with Murder* which airs on ABC. After a thirty-year absence from Broadway, Tyson returned with a role in Horton Foote's *The Trip to Bountiful*—She won the 2013 Tony Award for best performance by an actress in a leading role in a play.

William "Bill" Walker (1896–1992)

Best remembered for the role of Reverend Sykes in the classic film *To Kill a Mockingbird* (1962), Walker appeared in numerous television shows and films including *Goodyear Television Playhouse, Raintree County, Yancy Derringer, The Twilight Zone, Rawhide, Daniel Boone, Good Times, The Long, Hot Summer, Big Jake, What's Happening!!, Twilight's Last Gleaming*, and *The President's Plane is Missing*.

Douglas Turner Ward (1930–)

Douglas Turner Ward was born on May 5, 1930 in Burnside, Louisiana. He is an actor, known for *Man and Boy* (1971), *The Women of Brewster Place* (1989) and *For Love of Olivia* (2001).

Denzel Washington (1954–)

Academy award winner Denzel Washington is best known for his roles in several feature films, including *Malcolm X* (1992), *Training Day* (2001), and *American Gangster* (2007). Born in Mount Vernon, New York, on December 28, 1954, Denzel Washington first studied journalism at Fordham University but then discovered an interest in acting. He made his feature film debut in the comedy *A Carbon Copy* (1981) and was cast on the hit TV medical drama *St. Elsewhere* (1982–1988). He went on to appear in several blockbuster movies, including *Man on Fire*, *The Book of Eli*, *American Gangster*, *The Manchurian Candidate*, *Antwone Fisher*, *Remember the Titans*, *Philadelphia*, *Mo' Better Blues*, *He Got Game*, and won Oscars for his roles in *Glory* and *Training Day*. Denzel has done several films with Spike Lee.

Bert Williams (1874–1922)

Bert Williams is one of the first celebrated Black entertainers and Black Broadway stars in America. Dating back to the early 1900s, he is known for his performances in Blackface on stage and in film. Film Credits: *Fish* (1916); *A Natural Born Gambler, The Hon. Bert Williams, Walking Delegate* and *Lime Kiln Club Field Day* (1913).

Special Note: 100 Years in Post-Production: Resurrecting a Lost Landmark of Black Film History

From October 24, 2014–May 3, 2015 the Museum of Modern Art (MoMA) in New York, New York displayed an exhibit of unedited footage of an unreleased Black-cast feature film that showcased the work of Bert Williams—the film is titled *Lime Kiln Club Field Day* (1913). According to Museum of Modern Art's website:

> New York producers Klaw & Erlanger mounted the untitled project at virtually the same time that D. W. Griffith began his racist epic *The Birth of a Nation*, but they abandoned the seven reels of exposed film in postproduction, leaving buried within it unique photographic documentation of its black cast and white crew on the set.
> Starring the legendary Caribbean American musical theater performer and recording artist Bert Williams, the abandoned film also includes Harlem-based entertainment pioneers Sam Lucas, Abbie Mitchell, and J. Leubrie Hill, along with members of his Darktown

Follies stage company. Blending minstrel and contemporary performance styles in its telling of recycled race narratives, the work documents the effort by a community of virtuoso performers to achieve increased visibility in a time of segregation. (www.moma.org)

Spencer Williams (1893–1969)

Spencer Williams was an actor and filmmaker. He was best known for playing Andy in the *Amos 'n' Andy* television show that aired on CBS (1951–1953) and for directing the 1941 race film *The Blood of Jesus*. Williams along with Oscar Micheaux were early forerunners for African American film producers and directors.

Flip Wilson (1933–1998)

Geraldine said: "The Devil made me do it." Flip Wilson worked across the country as a comedian before garnering fame on programs like *The Tonight Show* and *Rowan and Martin's Laugh-In*. His own variety series *The Flip Wilson Show* launched in 1970 and was a ratings success airing on NBC. The show ended in 1974 ("Flip Wilson." Bio. A&E Television Networks, 2015. Web. 02 May 2015).

Oprah Winfrey (1954–)

Cited as the richest African American on the orb, billionaire Oprah Winfrey is best known for hosting her own internationally popular talk show from 1986 to 2011. She is an actress, philanthropist, publisher, and producer. In 1976, Oprah Winfrey hosted the TV chat show *People Are Talking*. The show became a hit and Winfrey remained a part of the staff for eight years before leaving to host her own morning show, *A.M. Chicago*. Her success as a talk show host led her to being cast as Sofia in Steven Spielberg's 1985 film *The Color Purple*. Winfrey was also nominated for an Academy Award for Best Supporting Actress.

In 1986 *The Oprah Winfrey Show* was launched nationally as a first-run syndicated program. The show was cleared in over one hundred markets with an audience size of 10 million people; gross revenues for the show were $125 million by the end of its first year (Oprah's estimated take home was thirty million). Her company Harpo Productions became the rights holder for the program which earned Winfrey even more money. In another effort to reach out to women, *Oxygen Media* (a company co-founded by Winfrey) was launched in 1999. *Oxygen* targets women 18+ with its cable and internet programming.

In 2009, Oprah Winfrey announced that she would be ending her program when her contract with ABC ended, in 2011. Soon after, she moved to her own network, *The Oprah Winfrey Network,* a joint venture with Discovery Communications ("Oprah Winfrey." Bio. A&E Television Networks, 2015. Web. 25 April 2015).

Appendix D

TEN HIGHEST-PAID BLACK TV ACTORS, ACTRESSES, AND
BROADCASTERS (2014)[1]

1. Robin Roberts, *Good Morning America*
   Salary: $14 million per year

2. Whoopi Goldberg, *The View*
   Salary: $5 million per year

3. Shemar Moore, *Criminal Minds*
   Salary: $175,000 per episode

4. Kerry Washington, *Scandal*
   Salary: $150,000 per episode

5. Don Cheadle, *House of Lies*
   Salary: $150,000 per episode

6. Andre Braugher, *Brooklyn Nine-Nine*
   Salary: $100,000 per episode

7. Anthony Anderson, *black*-ish
   Salary: $100,000 per episode

8. Jesse L. Martin, *The Flash*
   Salary: $100,000 per episode

9. Octavia Spencer, *Red Band Society*
   Salary: $75,000 per episode

10. Tracee Ellis Ross, *black*-ish
    Salary: $50,000 per episode

NOTE

1. Source: *TV Guide* September 2014.

Appendix E

TWO TOP BLACK PERFORMERS ANSWER QUESTIONS REGARDING
THE FUTURE OF BLACK REPRESENTATION IN FILM AND TV

Actor, Producer, and former NFL Football Player Jarrod Bunch

Question #1: No Black woman has ever been nominated for an Academy Award for Best Director. Additionally, no Black person has ever won an Academy for Best Director. Nominating *Selma* director Ava DuVernay for Best Director in 2015 could have sent a wonderful message—but it didn't happen. Moreover, there have only been three Black men nominated for best director: John Singleton for *Boyz n the Hood* (1991), Lee Daniels for *Precious* (2009), and Steve McQueen for *12 Years a Slave*; however, none of them won. Does the Academy really care about diversity? After all, African American Cheryl Boone Isaacs is president of the Academy of Motion Picture Arts and Sciences—should that make a difference?

JB: It's my opinion that the Academy's main concern is to oversee a finished product, rather than to advise as to what product should be made, and who makes it. The Academy defines its purpose as, "We recognize and uphold excellence in the motion picture arts and sciences, inspire imagination, and connect the world through the medium of motion pictures." I feel as if without pressure from the groups that feel neglected, the Academy will remain comfortable.

Question #2: What are your thoughts about television situation comedies that have titles such as *black*-ish and *Fresh Off the Boat*?

JB: I love *black*-ish. I have not seen *Fresh Off the Boat*. But in both shows, I think the titles evoke an expectation that creates an interest that would not have been present had the titles been more mainstream. Since the actors in *black*-ish and *Fresh Off the Boat* are different looking than the same recycled actors in many past shows, I understand why such a title. With the limited episode order networks give new sitcoms to find an audience, these shows have been forced to do things to attract an audience quickly.

Question #3: What has the controversy surrounding Bill Cosby done to the image and depiction of America's TV favorite dad, Cliff Huxtable?

JB: *The Cosby Show* will remain one of the greatest family shows of all time. Cliff Huxtable is a great character on that show. The things that Bill Cosby has been accused of will be hard to separate from Cliff, but it doesn't change how loved the head of that family unit is. The entire situation is sad.

ABC World News Tonight *correspondent Kendis Gibson*

Question #1: What are your thoughts regarding the progression (representation) of Black journalists on television?

KG: It's really come along quite a bit but still, no anchor has achieved the main anchor role in decades. I remember in the early 2000s it being a big deal at CNN when they had Frederika Whitfield and Leon Harris anchor a newscast together as fill in. . . . It was so rare to have two black anchors on the set together. Even though it was temporary it was a big deal. That said, I don't recall it happening many times since, at cable or broadcast. One step forward and sideways at the same time.

Question #2: No Black woman has ever been nominated for an Academy Award for Best Director. Additionally, no Black person has ever won an Academy for Best Director. Nominating *Selma* director Ava DuVernay for Best Director in 2015 could have sent a wonderful message—but it didn't happen. There have only been three Black men nominated for best director: John Singleton for *Boyz n the Hood* (1991), Lee Daniels for *Precious* (2009), and Steve McQueen for *12 Years a Slave*; none of them won. Does the Academy really care about diversity? After all, African American Cheryl Boone Isaacs is president of the Academy of Motion Picture Arts and Sciences—should that make a difference?

KG: It'll happen in due time. I don't tend to think of the academy as one collective body that thinks in the same mindset. So it's hard to say that an organization of many members cares either way about diversity. The Academy recognizes talent, and those good at marketing. Perhaps the directors aren't doing a good enough job at marketing.

Question #3: What are your thoughts about television situation comedies that have titles such as *black*-ish and *Fresh Off the Boat*?

KG: Completely politically incorrect and hilarious. We often make the same jokes at ourselves, why not watch them on TV?

Question #4: What has the controversy surrounding Bill Cosby done to the image and depiction of America's TV favorite dad, Cliff Huxtable?

KG: I think this is one for the history books still. It's disappointing that he didn't get ahead of this story. It almost seems like an admission of guilt. But still we will see what ends up happening with his reputation. It certainly has been very damaging.

Selected Bibliography

Adjaye, Joseph K. & Adrianne R. Andrews, ed. *Language, Rhythm, and Sound: Black Popular Cultures into the Twenty-First Century.* Pittsburgh: University of Pittsburgh Press, 1997. Print.

Anderson, Elijah. *Code of the Street: Decency, Violence, and the Moral Life of the Inner City.* New York: Norton, 1999. Print.

Appiah, Kwamw Anthony & Henry Louis Gates, Jr. *Africana Civil Rights: An A–Z Reference of the Movement That Changed America.* Philadelphia: Running Press, 2004. Print.

Blake, John. "Return of the Welfare Queen." CNN.com. 23 Jan. 2012. Web. 10 March 2014.

Berry, S. Torriano & Venise T. Berry. *The 50 Most Influential Black Films.* New York: Citadel, 2001. Print.

Berry, William. "The Relationship Double Bind: From Frustration To Enlightenment." *Psychology Today.* 11 August 2011. Web. 22 May 2015.

Bio. A&E Television Networks, 2015. Web. May–June 2015.

Bird, Sharon R. "Welcome to the Men's Club: Homosociality and the Maintenance of Hegemonic Masculinity." *Gender & Society* 10.2 (1996): 120–32. Print.

Blumberg, Antonia. *The World Of Vodou: Exhibit Brings To Life A Highly-Misunderstood Religion. The Huffington Post.* 14 October 2014. Web. 22 February 2015.

Bogle, Donald. *Toms, Coons, Mulattoes, Mamies, & Bucks.* New York: Continuum, 2006. Print.

Bowser, Pearl, Jane Gaines, & Charles Musser. *Oscar Micheaux and His Circle: African-American Filmmaking and Race Cinema of the Silent Era.* Bloomington: Indiana University Press, 2001. Print.

Braxton, Greg. "Next in line." *Los Angeles Times.com.* 30 March 2008. Web. 15 December 2014.

Butler, Judith. *Bodies That Matter: On the Discursive Limits of "Sex."* New York: Routledge, 1993. Print.

Caponi, Gina, ed. *Signifyin(g), Sanctifyin', and Slam Dunking: A Reader in African American Expressive Culture.* Print.

Collins, Lisa G. & Margo N. Crawford, eds. *New Thoughts on The Black Arts Movement.* New Brunswick, NJ: Rutgers University Press, 2006. Print.

Coward, Kyle. "When Hip-Hop First Went Corporate." *The Atlantic.com.* 21 April 2015. Web. 26 June 2015.

Cripps, Thomas. *Black Film as Genre.* Bloomington: Indiana University Press, 1978. Print.

———. *Slow Fade to Black: The Negro in American Film, 1900–1942.* New York: Oxford University Press, 1977. Print.

Davis, James F. *Who Is Black? One Nation's Definition.* University Park: Penn State University Press, 2001. Print.

Dent. Gina, ed. *Black Popular Culture: A Project by Michelle Wallace.* New York: Bay Press, 1992. Print.

Du Bois, W. E. B. *The Souls of Black Folks: Essays and Sketches.* Chicago: A. C. McClurg & Co., 1929. Print.

Dutchman. Directed by Anthony Harvey. Image Entertainment. 1967/1994. DVD.

Everett, Anna. *Returning the Gaze: A Genealogy of Black Film Criticism, 1909–1949.* Durham, NC: Duke University Press, 2001. Print.

Fischer, Lucy, ed. *Imitation of Life: Douglas Sirk, director; Lucy Fischer, editor*. New Brunswick, NJ: Rutgers University Press, 1991. Print.

Fishwick, Marshall. *Remus, Rastus, Revolution*. Bowling Green: Popular Press, 1971.

Gaines, Jane M. *Fire & Desire: Mixed-Race Movies in the Silent Era*. Chicago: University of Chicago Press, 2001. Print.

———. "'The Scar of Shame': Skin Color and Caste in Black Silent Melodrama." *Cinema Journal* 26 (1987): 3–21. Print.

Garber, Marjorie. *Vested Interests: Cross Dressing and Cultural Anxiety*. New York: Routledge, 1992. Print.

Gayle, Addison., ed. *The Black Aesthetic*. Garden City: Doubleday, 1972. Print.

Glasgow, D. G. *Black Underclass: Poverty, Unemployment and Entrapment of Ghetto Youth (The Jossey-Bass Social and Behavioral Science Series)*. San Francisco: Jossey-Bass, 1980. Print.

Hall, Stuart. *Different*. London: Phaidon, 2002. Print.

———. "Encoding, decoding." *The Cultural Studies Reader*. Edited by Simon During. New York: Routledge, 1993. Print.

———. *Representation: Cultural Representations and Signifying Practices*. Thousand Oaks, CA: Sage Publication, 1997. Print.

———. "What is This 'Black' in Black Popular Culture?" *Social Justice* 20.1–2 (1993): 104–13. Print.

———, & Paul du Gay, eds. *Questions of Cultural Identity*. Thousand Oaks, CA: Sage Publication, 1996. Print.

Harrell, Camara Jules P. *Manichean Psychology : Racism and the Minds of People of African Descent*. Washington, DC: Howard University Press, 1999. Print.

Hatch, V. James & Ted Shine. *Black Theater USA*. New York: The Free Press, 1996.

Historical Encyclopedia 1–2 (1993): Web. 05 April. 2008.

hooks, bell. *Black Looks: Race and Representation*. Boston: South End Press, 1992. Print.

———. *Outlaw Culture: Resisting Representations*. New York: Routledge, 1994. Print.

Hurst, Fannie. *Imitation of Life*. Cleveland: The World Publishing Co., 1933. Print.

Imitation of Life. Directed by Douglas Sirk. Universal 1959/2003. DVD

Jaynes, Gerald D., ed. *Encyclopedia of African American Society*. Thousand Oaks, CA: Sage Publication, 2005. Print.

Johnson, E. Patrick. *Appropriating Blackness: Performance and the Politics of Authenticity*. Durham, NC: Duke University Press, 2003. Print.

Jones, LeRoi (Amiri Baraka). *Dutchman*. New York: Harper Perennial, 1971. Print.

Kane, Joe. *Night of the Living Dead: Behind the Scenes of the Most Terrifying Zombie Movie Ever*. New York: Kensington Publishing, 2010.

Kapsch, Joseph. *Viola Davis Defies Hollywood Stereotypes as She Keeps it Real: 'I Didn't Want to Be the Vogue Woman.'* Video. TheWrap.com. Web. 29 Jun. 2015.

Keegan, Rebecca. "USC study: Minorities still under-represented in popular films." *Los Angeles Times*. 30 October 30 2013. Web. 19 February 2014.

King James Version (KJV). Bible Gateway. Web. 5 Jan. 2014.

Klotman, Phyllis R. "About Black Film . . ." *Black American Literature Forum* 12 (1978): 123–27. Print.

Korkis, Jim. *Who's Afraid of the Song of the South? And Other Forbidden Disney Stories*. Orlando: Theme Park Press, 2012. Print.

Kumar, N. Nita. "The Logic of Retribution: Amiri Baraka's Dutchman." *African American Review*." October 2003. Web. 24 November 2014.

Lott, Eric. "Love and Theft: The Racial Unconsciousness of Blackface Minstrelsy." *Representations* 39 (1992): 23–50. Print.

———. *Love & Theft: Blackface Minstrelsy and the American Working Class (Race and American Culture)*. New York: Oxford University Press, 2013. Print

Lott, Tommy. *The Invention of Race: Black Culture and the Politics of Representation*. Malden, MA: Blackwell, 1999. Print.

Lusane, Clarence. *Race in the Global Era: African Americans at the Millennium*. Boston: South End Press, 1997. Print.

MacDonald, Fred J. *Blacks and White TV: African Americans in Television Since 1948,* 2nd ed. Chicago: Nelson-Hall Publishers, 1992. Print.

McAlister, Elizabeth A. "Vodou: Haitian Religion." *Encyclopedia Britannica Online.* 2015. Web. 03 May 2015.

McGruder, Aaron. "Interview by Cynthia McFadeen." *Nightline.* ABC. WABC, New York. 17 January 2006. Television.

Means Coleman, Robin R. *African American Viewers and the Black Situation Comedy: Situating Racial Humor.* New York: Garland Publishers, 1998/2000. Print.

Mills, Charles. *The Racial Contract.* Ithaca, NY: Cornell University Press, 1997. Print.

Naison, Mark. "Outlaw Culture," *Reconstruction* 1, no. 4 (1994): 128. Print.

———. *White Boy: A Memoir.* Philadelphia: Temple University Press, 2002. Print.

Napier, Winston. *African American Literary Theory: A Reader.* New York: New York University Press, 2000. Print.

Neal, Mark Anthony. *Soul Babies: Black Popular Culture and the Post-Soul Aesthetic.* New York: Routledge, 2002. Print.

Negrospirituals.com. www.negrospirituals.com/. Web. 22 January 2016.

Nelson, Angela M. S. "The Repertoire of Black Popular Culture." *Americana: The Journal of American Popular Culture (1900–present)* 8.1 (Spring 2009): Web. 08 February 2015.

———. "Black Situation Comedies and the Politics of Television Art." *Cultural Diversity and the U.S. Media.* Edited by Yahya R. Kamalipour and Theresa Carilli. Albany: State University of New York Press, 1998. Print.

New English Translation (NET Bible). Bible Gateway. Web. 31 Jul. 2015.

Peterson, Eugene H. *The Message (MSG).* Colorado Springs, CO: NavPress, 2002. Bible Gateway. Web. 1 Jul. 2015.

Regester, Charles. *Black Entertainers in African AMerican Newspaper Articles, Volume 1: An Annotated Bibliography of The Chicago Defender, The Afro-American (Baltimore), and The New York Amsterdam News, 1910–1950, annotated edition.* Jefferson, NC: McFarland, 2002. Print.

Rogin, Michael. "'Democracy and Burnt Cork': The End of Blackface, the Beginning of Civil Rights." *Representations* 46 (1994): 1–34. Print.

Shakur, Sanyika (aka Kody Scott). *Monster: The Autobiography of an L. A. Gang Member.* New York: Grove Press, 1993. Print.

Shaw, Harry B., ed. *Perspectives of Black Popular Culture.* Bowling Green: Popular Press, 1990.

Sheehy, John. "The Mirror and the Veil: The Passing Novel and the Quest for American Racial Identity-Critical Essay." *African American Review.* 3 November 2005. Print.

Smith, Stacey L., Marc Choueiti, Elizabeth Scofield, & Katherine Pieper. *Gender Inequality in 500 Popular Films: Examining On-Screen Portrayals and Behind-the-Scenes Employment Patterns in Motion Pictures Released between 2007–2012.* Annenberg School for Communication & Journalism University of Southern California. Web. 19 February 2016.

Stam, Robert. *Film Theory: An Introduction.* Malden, MA: Blackwell Publishers, 1999. Print.

The Black Power Mixtape: 1965–1975 (2010). Dir. Göran Olsson. Web. 9 Aug. 2014.

The Johns Hopkins Guide to Literary Theory and Criticism. Baltimore: Johns Hopkins University Press. 1993. Print.

The Voice. Nashville, TN: Thomas Nelson, 2012. Bible Gateway. Web. 25 Feb. 2016.

Theoharis, Jeanne. *The Rebellious Life of Mrs. Rosa Parks.* Boston: Beacon Press, 2013. Print.

Verney, Kevern. *African Americans and US Popular Culture (Introductions to History).* New York: Routledge, 2003. Print.

Wallace, Maurice O. *Constructing the Black Masculine: Identity and Ideality in African American Men's Literature and Culture, 1775–1995.* Durham, NC: Duke University Press, 2002. Print.

Walters, Suzanna Danuta. *Lives Together, Worlds Apart: Mothers and Daughters in Popular Culture*. Berkeley: University of California Press, 1992. Print.

Weisenfeld, Judith. *Hollywood Be Thy Name: African American Religion in American Film, 1929–1949*. Berkeley: University of California Press, 2007. Print.

Williams, Terry Tempest. *Crackhouse: Notes from the End of the Line*. New York: Penguin Books, 1992/1993. Print.

Wilson, Julius William. *More than Just Race: Being Black and Poor in the Inner City (Issues of Our Time)*. New York: W. W. Norton & Company, 2010. Print.

Witcover, Jules. *The Year the Dream Died: Revisiting 1968 in America*. New York: Warner Books, 1997. Print.

Wolf, George & Harry J. Elam, Jr. "Signifyin(g) on African-American Theatre: The Colored Museum by George Wolf." *Theatre Journal* 44 (1992): 291–303. Print.

Worthen, W. B. *The Wadsworth Anthology of Drama Fourth Edition*. Boston: Thompson Wadsworth, 2004. Print.

X, Malcolm. "Message to the Grass Roots." Northern Grass Roots Leadership Conference. King Solomon Baptist Church, Detroit. 10 November 1963. Address. *Teaching American History.org*. Web. 02 February 2015.

Index

About the Author

David L. Moody is an assistant professor in the Department of Communication Studies at the State University of New York at Oswego (SUNY Oswego). He is the author of *Political Melodies in the Pews?: The Voice of the Black Christian Rapper in the Twenty-First-Century Church*, which is published by Lexington Books (September 2012). He received the Harry Shaw Award for his work on African American visual popular culture from the Popular Culture Association/American Culture Association in 2014.